# SNAZZY JARS

# SNAZZY JARS

## Glorious Gift Ideas

Marie Browning

Sterling Publishing Co., Inc.
New York

## Prolific Impressions Production Staff:

Editor in Chief: Mickey Baskett
Copy Editor: Phyllis Mueller
Graphics: Dianne Miller, Karen Turpin
Styling: Lenos Key
Photography: Jerry Mucklow
Administration: Jim Baskett

Every effort has been made to insure that the information presented is accurate. Since we have no control over physical conditions, individual skills, or chosen tools and products, the publisher disclaims any liability for injuries, losses, untoward results, or any other damages which may result from the use of the information in this book. Thoroughly read the instructions for all products used to complete the projects in this book, paying particular attention to all cautions and warnings shown for that product to ensure their proper and safe use.

Library of Congress Cataloging-in-Publication Data

Browning, Marie.
  Snazzy jars : glorious gift ideas / Marie Browning.
      p. cm.
  Includes index.
  ISBN-13: 978-1-4027-3158-7
  ISBN-10: 1-4027-3158-2
  1.  Handicraft. 2.  Storage jars. 3.  Decoration and ornament. I. Title.
  TT157.B7874 2006
  745.5--dc22

                                                                    2005034550

10 9 8 7 6 5 4 3 2

Published by Sterling Publishing Co., Inc.
387 Park Avenue South, New York, N.Y. 10016
©2006 by Prolific Impressions, Inc.
Produced by Prolific Impressions, Inc.
160 South Candler St., Decatur, GA 30030
Distributed in Canada by Sterling Publishing
c/o Canadian Manda Group, 165 Dufferin Street
Toronto, Ontario, Canada M6K 3H6
Distributed in the United Kingdom by GMC Distribution Services,
Castle Place, 166 High Street, Lewes, East Sussex, England BN7 1XU
Distributed in Australia by Capricorn Link (Australia) Pty. Ltd.
P.O. Box 704, Windsor, NSW 2756 Australia

Printed in China

Sterling  ISBN-13: 978-1-4027-3158-7
          ISBN-10: 1-4027-3158-2

For information about custom editions, special sales, premium and corporate purchases, please contact Sterling Special Sales Department at 800-805-5489 or specialsales@sterlingpub.com.

## Acknowledgments

I like to recommend supporting local craft, art supply, and hardware stores whenever possible, but because not every store can carry everything I have provided information on the manufacturers of the products used in this book so you can find out where they distribute their wares near you. Their websites contain technical product support and other useful information as well.

I thank these manufacturers for their generous contributions of quality products and support in the creation of the projects.

*For glass jars, canning jars, and reproduction antique jars:* Alltrista Corporation, Indianapolis, Indiana, USA, www.alltrista.com

*For general craft glues, including Gem-Tack and Fabri-Tac:* Beacon Adhesives, Mt. Vernon, New York, USA, www.beaconadhesive.com

*For ribbons and trims:* Berwick-Offray LLC, Chester, New Jersey, USA, www.offray.com

*For opaque and transparent PermEnamel paints for glass and stencils:* Delta Technical Coatings, Whittier, California, USA, www.deltacrafts.com

*For two-part resin coating, Envirotex Lite:* Environmental Technologies, Fields Landing, California, USA, www.eti-usa.com

*For scissors, rotary cutter, and general tools:* Fiskars Brands, Inc., Wausau, Wisconsin, USA, www.fiskars.com

*For vintage peel and stick labels and jar lamp kits:* Heart & Home Collectibles, Inc., Ajax, Ontario, Canada, www.melissafrances.com

*For acrylic high gloss enamel paint for glass, decoupage medium, transparent glass paint and liquid leading, Paint for Plastic, Papier paints, All Night Media Rubber Stamps, and stencils:* Plaid Enterprises Inc., Norcross, Georgia, USA, www.plaidonline.com

*For Sculpey and Premo brands of polymer clay and polymer clay tools:* Polyform Products, Elk Grove Village, Illinois, USA, www.sculpey.com

*For paint brushes, sponges, and rub-on transfers:* Royal Brush, Merrillville, Indiana, USA, www.royalbrush.com

# About the Author

Marie Browning is a consummate craft designer who has made a career of designing products, writing books and articles, and teaching and demonstrating. You may have been charmed by her creative acumen but not been aware of the woman behind it; she has designed stencils, stamps, transfers, and a variety of other award-winning product lines for art and craft supply companies.

Marie Browning also has written numerous books on creative living, and her articles and designs have appeared in myriad home decor and crafts magazines. She earned a Fine Arts Diploma from Camosun College and attended the University of Victoria. A Certified Professional Demonstrator, she is a design member of the Crafts and Hobby Association (CHA) and a board member of the Society of Craft Designers (SCD). Marie also is on the trend committee for SCD that researches and writes about upcoming trends in the arts and crafts industry. In 2004, Marie was selected by *Craftrends* trade publication as a "Top Influential Industry Designer."

She lives, gardens, and crafts on Vancouver Island in Canada. She and her husband Scott have three children: Katelyn, Lena, and Jonathan. Marie can be contacted at www.mariebrowning.com.

## Books by Marie Browning
## Published by Sterling

*Jazzy Gift Baskets* (2005)
*Purse Pizzazz* (2005)
*Really Jazzy Jars* (2005)
*Totally Cool Polymer Clay for Kids* (2005)
*Totally Cool Soapmaking for Kids* (2004, reprinted in softcover)
*Wonderful Wraps* (2003, reprinted in softcover)
*Jazzy Jars* (2003, reprinted in softcover)
*Designer Soapmaking* (2003, reprinted in German)
*300 Recipes for Soap* (2002, reprinted in softcover and in French)
*Crafting with Vellum and Parchment* (2001, reprinted in softcover with the title *New Paper Crafts*)
*Melt & Pour Soapmaking (2000, reprinted in softcover)*
Hand Decorating Paper (2000, reprinted in softcover)
*Memory Gifts* (2000, reprinted in softcover with the title *Family Photocrafts*)
*Making Glorious Gifts from Your Garden* (1999, reprinted in softcover)
*Handcrafted Journals, Albums, Scrapbooks & More* (1999, (reprinted in softcover)
*Beautiful Handmade Natural Soaps* (1998, reprinted in softcover with the title *Natural Soapmaking*)

# Contents

remember when...

Cheers!

I have filled this book with new jar projects crafted with popular decorative techniques. It contains more than 40 projects using canning jars, storage jars, and recycled jars to make economical gifts and practical storage canisters. There's information about supplies, step-by-step instructions for the decorating techniques, and a section filled with ideas for decorating lids and making creative tags and labels.

I have lots of ideas for using your decorated jars!
Decorated jars can adorn any room in the house to organize and store bits and pieces. You can fill them with layered food mixes or use them to hold treats like cookies and crackers or as canisters for kitchen storage. Smaller jars are perfect for spare change, pencil holders, or desk storage.

# What can you do with a jar?

You'll find a wealth of ideas to get your creative juices flowing, like easy painted and stenciled jars and decoupage projects with paper and fabric for both novice and experienced crafters. I've included jars with mosaic decorations using glass and mirrors, ideas for decorating jars with polymer clay and resin-coated embellishments, photo collage memory jars, and creative characters from felt and plastic foam that are fun to make for kids of all ages. There's also a section of recipes and ideas for what to put in your decorated jars.

Why not gather friends and family and have a jar party! Ask everyone to bring a dozen clean canning jars, and tell them to plan to spend a fun day decorating them and creating layered mixes.

Of course, decorated jars make wonderful gifts. They're a great way to extend thanks or sympathy, to remember a special occasion, or to celebrate a birthday, a graduation, a new baby, or a new house. When you give a jar, be prepared for heartfelt thanks from the recipient for the gift of your creativity and time.

*Marie Browning*

# jar toppers

# character jars

# tags & labels

# memory jars

9

# About Jars

The major companies that manufacture canning jars today - Ball, Mason, and Kerr - were all started at least 100 years ago. Jars used for home canning are called "Mason jars" after John L. Mason, who invented and patented the design for canning jars. Old Mason jars were made of blue glass and today are prized by collectors. Mason's patent expired in 1875.

The Ball brothers, Frank and Edmund, founded the Ball Corporation in 1880. They started with a wood-jacketed tin container for paint and varnish and soon expanded into the home-canning field.

Today, Ball produces glass canning jars as well as space systems and electro-optic materials. The Kerr Company, founded in 1902, developed the now-familiar two-piece lid.

## Types of Jars

I like to collect jars all year so I have a nice selection on hand when I wish to create a gift.

**Mason-Style Canning Jars** come in half-pint, pint, quart, and half-gallon sizes with a standard or wide opening (the "mouth"). The glass jars may be

10

embossed with fruit motifs, diamond patterns, or company names and crests. Because of the popularity of decorating jars, a plain glass - perfect for painting and decorating - is now available. They're easy to find at grocery, hardware, and housewares stores.

**Decorative Glass Storage Jars** are a pleasure to decorate and use for storage and gift giving. They provide an inexpensive surface for all the creative techniques presented in this book. Look for them at crafts, kitchen and bath, and container stores.

**Old-fashioned Wire Bail Jars** cost a little more but give the finished project a sophisticated appearance. They are made in many sizes and shapes and can be found at quality kitchen stores and department stores.

**Apothecary Jars** are a great choice for elegant designs for the bathroom and bedroom. They are generally straight-sided glass jars topped with a glass or metal lid. Many have plastic seals and are air-tight.

**Recycled Jars** that once contained baby food, mayonnaise, and spaghetti sauce are some of my favorites. They offer smooth sides (no embossed motifs) that are great for decorating. Soak them in water to remove the labels and clean them carefully. Many lids with printing can be covered with metal paints and fabric tops. Recycled jars are not recommended for canning foods.

**Antique Canning Jars** are very beautiful but are also more brittle and easier to break. Check old jars carefully for chips or imperfections. Some old jars are very valuable - early colored glass canning jars have sold for up to $1,000 each - so if you're not sure of the value of an old jar, it's wiser not to use it. Instead, look for **reproductions of antique jars** - they have the vintage look for a fraction of the price.

## Lids for Jars

Typical canning jar lids come in two parts - a flat lid and a screw-on band. Wire-bail jars have glass lids and, often, rubber gaskets. Storage jars typically come with plastic screw-top lids; one-piece metal screw-top lids are generally used by food manufacturers. They are safe to re-use when sealing is not required. You can also use wooden stoppers (some have rubber seals) and natural corks for jars.

## Caring for Decorated Jars

Follow these tips for long-lasting jars:
- Handle with care. Glass is fragile.
- Do not expose jars to extreme hot or cold temperatures.
- Do not immerse decorated jars in hot water, and do not leave decorated jars standing in water.
- For lasting color, spray the decorated jar with a sealer. Choose from matte, satin, and gloss finishes.
- To clean a decorated jar, simply wipe with a soft, damp cloth. Jars with a resin coating are more durable - they will withstand moisture and can be used as a vase or outdoors.

---

### EMBELLISHING JARS

Embellishments make jars look professional and finished. These are some of my favorites. You can make them or find them at your favorite craft outlet.

- **Beads**
  Beautiful glass beads can be threaded on thin elastic cords to make "jar jewelry." Inexpensive beaded trims are easy to find and available in a great variety of lengths and colors.

- **Charms**
  Charms are available in a wide range of metallic finishes and motifs. Use a silicone-based glue designed for metal to adhere charms to jars and lids.

- **Plastic Novelty Buttons**
  Plastic buttons come in a wide range of theme motifs. Use wire cutters to remove the shanks before adhering them with a silicone-based glue.

- **Ribbons, Braid & Trims**
  Ribbons, braids, and trims are very easy to use and coordinate with a project. A huge variety of widths, colors, and textures await your creative touch.

- **Metal Label Holders**
  Metal label holders are widely available at scrapbooking and crafts stores. I glue the metal frames to the jars using strong metal glue and attach flat-head eyelets to the screw holes in the frames for a finished look. Cut card paper to size and slip in the metal frame to label your creations.

# JAR TOPPERS

Sometimes all a jar needs is a fancy top and a matching tag or label. The lid and tag can create a mood (romantic, fun, charming) or embody a decorating style (Victorian, whimsical, classical). My favorite decorative treatments include paper, fabric, and lace. The designs in this section show an array of inspiring possibilities.

# Fabric-Topped Lids

Fabric is an easy, traditional topper for jar gifts. With simple trims and embellishments, your jars go from ordinary to extraordinary. You can cut the fabric with pinking or scalloping shears, bind or trim the edges, make a narrow hem, or (for squares) fray the edges to make a fringe.

## Basic Supplies for Fabric Lids

**Fabric**, cotton or cotton-polyester blends, 6" to 7" squares or circles

**Lace doilies**

**Trims** - Buttons, lace, ribbons

**Adhesives** - Hot glue gun and clear glue sticks, white fabric glue

*Optional:* **Polyester batting**, for a puffy lid

## Basic Instructions for Fabric-Topped Lids

1. *Option:* For a puffy top, use the flat lid as a template and cut a piece of batting. Use a glue gun to glue the batting to the top of the lid.
2. *Option:* Finish the edge of the fabric. (See above.)
3. Place the flat lid on the jar. Center a square or circle of fabric on the lid.
4. Twist on the metal band to hold everything in place.
5. Using the glue gun, add trims and embellishments. ❑

*Pictured right:* Fall Leaves Seasonal Jar. Instructions begin on page 36.

# Fabric Glued to Metal Lids

Gluing fabric on the jar top is a perfect match for a fabric-covered jar - you can cover the flat lid only or both the lid and the band. This favorite technique is a colorful and lasting treatment that can be further embellished with buttons and ribbons.

## Basic Instructions for Glued-Fabric Lids

*To cover a flat lid:*

1. Using the flat lid as a template, cut out a circle of fabric.
2. Coat the flat metal lid with fabric glue. Press the fabric in place, smoothing any wrinkles. Let dry.
3. Brush with a coat of white glue to finish. Let dry.

*To cover the metal band:*

1. Cut a strip of fabric as long as the circumference of the band plus 1/2" and as wide as the width of the band plus 1".
2. Coat the band (including the top edge) with white glue.
3. Press the strip of fabric over the glue. Using scissors, cut slits in the top edge of the fabric at 1/4" intervals. (This allows smooth coverage of the top edge of the band.) Let dry.
4. Coat the fabric with white glue. Let dry. ❏

# Fabric Glued to Plastic Lids

Plastic lids also can be covered with fabric.
It's easy to stretch and gather the fabric
to fit around the lid.

## Basic Instructions for Plastic Lids

1. Cut a circle of fabric to fit over the top and sides of the lid plus 1".
2. Coat the plastic lid with white glue. Center the fabric on the lid and press into the glue, stretching the fabric over the edge and around the sides of the lids. Let dry.
3. Trim excess fabric from the bottom of the lid.
4. Coat the fabric with white glue. Add ribbon, cording, or trim to the bottom edge of the lid to hide the cut edge of the fabric. Let dry. ❑

# Lacy Lids

Lacy crocheted doilies and lace trims lend a romantic touch to jar lids. You can buy new doilies or look for antique ones at thrift shops and tag sales. (I regularly find them for less than a dollar each.) I especially like doilies with linen centers and am always on the lookout for clean ones in good condition.

Fill these romantic jars with homemade bath salts, bath soaps, homemade chocolates, or favorite layered cookie mixes.

## Basic Instructions for Lacy Lids

*For puffy fabric-topped lids with lace trim:*

1. Cut a piece of batting and glue to the top of a plastic lid.
2. Cut a circle of fabric and cover the lid, following the instructions on the previous page.
3. Trim the edge of the lid by gluing lace on the edge.
4. Cut a piece of 1/4" wide satin ribbon the circumference of the lid plus 20". Glue the ribbon around the jar, leaving 10" tails.
5. Tie ends in a bow. Glue a button (with shank removed) on the knot of the bow to finish the lid. ❑

*For crocheted doily-topped lids:*

1. Determine the finished size of the doily. If you need to cut the doily, apply a line of white glue to where you plan to cut. Let the glue dry completely, then cut. (The glue prevents unraveling.)
2. Place the doily over the lid. There are a number of options:

   **Doily secured with a metal band** - Put the doily over the flat lid, then screw the band in place.

   **Doily used for a removable lace collar** - Cut the fabric center from the doily and glue to the flat metal lid. Glue lace trim to the top of the band. To make the lace collar, thread the remaining piece of the doily with satin ribbon and place the collar around the band, gathering it on the ribbon to fit. Tie a bow to secure. (The lace collar can be removed for easy opening of the jar.)

**Doily threaded with ribbon** - Install the lid and band on the jar. Position the doily on the jar. Thread ribbon through the doily or wrap with ribbon and tie around the neck of the jar.

**Doily with fabric center** - (good for doilies with fabric damaged centers) Cover a white plastic storage lid with white glue. Thread ribbon through the doily, place it on lid, and pull the ribbon to gather the doily around the lid and knot. Cut a fabric top to size with pinking shears and glue to the center top of the lid to hide the damage.

*Option:* Thread an additional piece of ribbon through the doily to attach a tag. ❏

# TAGS & LABELS
## for Jars

Fabric tags and labels make a nice addition to fabric decoupaged jars.
Many beautiful fabric labels are available at craft and fabric stores.
Designing your own fabric tags and labels is a great way to use
leftover bits and pieces!

## Basic Supplies for Fabric Labels & Tags

**Tags** - Tag template, card paper, and shape cutter *or* pre-cut paper tags; wooden tags; fabric labels *or* card paper and fabric

**Tools** - Hole punches *or* awl, eyelets and eyelet setter, scissors, craft knife

**Trims** - Ribbon, elastic cord, raffia

**Adhesives** - Hot glue gun and clear glue sticks, white fabric glue

**Permanent pens or markers**, for labeling

## Basic Instructions for Fabric Labels

*Using purchased fabric labels:*
1. Use white glue to attach the label.
2. Add a coat of white glue to protect and finish the label. Let dry completely.
3. Use a permanent pen to add lettering.

*Making fabric labels:*
1. Cut rectangles or squares from fabric.
2. Glue to jars with white glue.
3. Add a coat of white glue to protect and finish the label. Let dry completely.
4. Use a permanent pen to add lettering. ❏

## Basic Instructions for Fabric-Covered Paper Tags

1. Completely cover a piece of card weight paper with a very thin layer of white glue. Press the fabric over the glue to laminate the fabric to the paper. Let dry completely.
2. Use a tag template to trace a tag outline on the paper side.
3. Cut out the tag with plain or decorative edge scissors.
4. Punch a hole at the top of the tag. Add an eyelet to finish.
5. *Decorative options:* Fray the fabric at the bottom of the tag to make a fringe. Glue on additional embellishments with a glue gun.
6. Use a permanent black pen to add lettering to the paper back of the tag. ❏

## Basic Instructions for Covering Wooden Tags

1. Cut a piece of fabric 1/2" larger than the tag.
2. Coat the tag with white glue. Place the fabric on top and press into the glue, smoothing out any wrinkles.
3. Coat the fabric with white glue. Let dry completely.
4. Place the tag, fabric side down, on a cutting mat. Trim away the excess fabric with a craft knife.
5. Use a glue gun to attach additional embellishments.
6. Using an awl, poke a hole through the fabric over the hole in the wooden tag. Glue in an eyelet to finish.
7. Use a permanent pen to add lettering to the back of the tag. ❏

# Paper Topped Lids & Tags

I like to use scraps of paper to cover lids and create labels and tags. For tags, I use card weight paper with layered paper panels. A tag template with a shape cutter is a great tool for cutting tags from decorative paper; you can make lots of tags easily. Use a variety of hole punch shapes and eyelets for attaching the tag to the jar with elastic cord or decorative fibers.

## Basic Supplies for Paper Tags & Lids

**Papers** - Decorative papers, card papers, self-adhesive labels

**Trims and embellishments** - Border stickers, strips of matching paper, accent stickers, rub-on motifs, novelty buttons, ribbons, decorative fibers, elastic cord, raffia

**Cutting tools** - Paper trimmer, decorative edge scissors, tag template and shape cutter

**Punches** - Decorative hole punches, eyelets and eyelet setter

**Labeling tools** - Felt markers, gel pens

**Adhesives** - White glue, hot glue gun with clear glue sticks

## Basic Instructions

*For paper-topped lids:*

1. Using the lid as a template, cut a circle from decorative paper or card paper. Cut six tiny slits into the circle approximately 1" apart. (The slits allow the paper circle to be glued on top of the flat lid without creasing.)
2. Glue the paper circle to the flat lid. Let dry.
3. Use a 1/2" wide strip of paper, a border sticker, or ribbon to decorate the band. Use white glue or a glue gun to adhere. *Option:* To cover the band and its top edge, cut a wider strip of paper. Use white glue to attach the paper strip around the band. Using scissors, cut slits in the top of the paper about 1/4" apart. The paper will wrap around the top of the band and over the edge smoothly.
4. Accent further with stickers, rub-on motifs, or novelty buttons (shanks removed).

*For paper tags and labels:*

TIP: When using a lightweight decorative paper for a tag, glue it to a piece of heavier card paper.

1. Use decorative edge scissors to cut out tags and labels.
2. Accent tags with decorative stickers or novelty buttons.
3. Punch holes with decorative punches.
4. Add lettering or greetings to tags with gel pens or felt-tipped pens.
5. Use ribbon, cord, or raffia to attach the tag and tie around the jar neck. ❏

# Self-Adhesive Labels

There are a wide variety of pre-printed labels available to decorate your jars and gift tags. Before applying them, make sure your jar surface is clean and grease free. Some labels need to wrap around the jar and stick to themselves to prevent the label from pulling away from the jar.

You can design your own labels with photographs and printed motifs on double-sided adhesive paper or a laminating machine. This is especially handy if you're making and decorating lots of jars as gifts or to sell.

*Pictured above:* A photograph was cut to fit the lid; a piece of clear acetate protects the photo. Matching satin ribbon was glued around the band and decorated with a beaded sticker. The jar was further accented with a beaded bracelet and a matching tag. Use the jar to hold a small beading kit or a food gift.

*Pictured above, left:*
## Bath Time Jar

For a jar filled with Baby Yourself Bath Salts, I chose yellow gingham paper to cover the flat lid and the matching tag. Rainbow ribbon wraps the band and is used to attach the tag. Bath-motif novelty buttons embellish the top and the tag.

*Pictured above, right:*
## Blue & Yellow Baby Gift Jar

Decorative paper covers the flat lid, and yellow grosgrain ribbon and blue rickrack decorate the band. Novelty buttons are glued to the top. The matching tag is embellished with stickers and a novelty button. Fill this jar with baby biscuits or baby soothers.

## Garden Jar

Seeds or plant markers can be placed in this jar, which makes a welcomed gift for a friend who loves to garden. Fabric stickers in fun flower colors (purple and pink) cover the flat lid, the metal band, and a wooden tag. Silver-colored garden charms decorate the tag and lid.

*Pictured above, left:*
# Kisses Jar

The inspiration for this jar came from matching tags and decorative papers I found at my local scrapbooking store. The decorative paper covers both the flat lid and the band - if you can't find this paper, photocopy the cover of a romantic novel and use it to reproduce the theme. I used red satin ribbon to attach a novelty lock and key and a layered paper tag. Fill the jar with (what else?) chocolate kisses for a thoughtful thank-you!

*Pictured above, right:*
# Candy Jar

Brightly colored paper and fun plastic novelties decorate the jar top. I used white glue to adhere ribbon around the band and attached the tag with decorative fibers. Fill the jar with colorful candies for a sweet, fun gift.

## Travel Bank Jar

I painted the band with acrylic paints for metals (dark green and terra cotta) and used the flat metal lid as a template to cut a circle from a piece of mat board, which I covered with map-motif paper. I used a craft knife to carefully cut a slot in the mat board lid and outlined the slot with a black pen. I glued the mat board circle inside the band with white glue. Travel stickers embellish the lid and cover the plastic tags that were tied around the neck of the jar with green grosgrain ribbon. Fill the jar with spare change to go towards your next vacation!

*Pictured on the left:*

## Cork Tassel Jar

I made a tassel from a recycled wine bottle cork by gluing glass beads to the top and bottom and using fibers to make the tassel fringe and top tie. The jar's flat lid and band are covered with coordinating decorative papers. The tag is decorated with a cork-motif sticker and tied around the jar neck with wine-colored satin ribbon. Fill this jar with homemade cheese biscuits and present it with a bottle of your favorite wine.

*Pictured on the right:*

## Classic Jar

This classic-design jar could hold all kinds of food gifts - I especially like to use it for soup mixes. The flat lid is covered with decorative paper and adorned with black satin ribbon and a polymer clay seal. The band is covered with polymer clay and textured with a rubber stamp. After baking and cooling, I rubbed the band with dark brown acrylic paint for an antique look. The tag is decorated with paper, stickers, and a brass charm.

*Pictured on the left:*

# Butterfly Jar

The flat lid and band are covered with shiny metallic stickers, and the tag is embellished with coordinating metallic lettering and border stickers. Use this simple jar to hold a gift of chocolates or a favorite drink mix.

*Pictured on the right:*

# Honey Bee Jar

The bee-themed decorations make this jar the perfect container for homemade spiced honey. The flat top is covered with decorative paper, and the band is wrapped with gold raffia. A copper bee charm embellishes the knot. A matching tag is covered with bee-themed stickers.

# PAINTED JARS

Paints suitable for glass are available in a wide range of colors and include opaque, transparent, and dimensional paints. Acrylic paints suitable for glass also can be used on plastic jars.

## Acrylic Enamels

Durable, glossy acrylic paints for glass come in a variety of pre-mixed colors in convenient squeeze bottles. Do not thin these paints with water - use a blending medium or thinning medium manufactured for the brand of paint you're using. While wet, the paints clean up easily with soap and water. When dry and cured, the painted jars can be baked in your home oven, yielding a durable painted surface that is waterproof. Follow the paint manufacturer's instructions for curing and baking. Allow the jar to cool before removing it from the oven. After baking, some paints are top-rack dishwasher safe. Hand wash painted jars for best results.

## Transparent Paints

Acrylic transparent paints are used to create faux glass stained effects on glass that are especially nice for candle jars. The paints are packaged in handy squeeze tubes for easy application and come in a wide range of colors.

## Paint Pens

Paint pens come in many colors and in fine, medium, and calligraphy chisel point tips. Use them to add accents on jars or for details on painted jars. If you're using a paint pen over another paint, be sure the paint is dry and fully cured before using the paint pen, and always test the pen to be sure it's compatible with the other paint.

(TIP: Use the bottom of the jar.) Follow the manufacturer's instructions for priming the pen and starting the flow of paint to the nib.

## Brushes

You need a variety of good-quality artist's brushes:

**Flats** - 1/2" and 1", for basecoating and painting large motifs and #4, #6, and #10 for general painting and details

**Rounds** - #1 and #4, for general painting and details

**Liners** - #1, #0, #00, for fine detailing

## Sponges

Use fine-textured sea sponges for basecoating and sponged finishes and dense foam sponges (the type used for applying make-up) for stenciling.

## Basic Painting Supplies

You will need these supplies for painted jar projects:

**Paper towels**, for holding the pattern inside the jar

**Water basin** , for rinsing brushes

**Low tack ("painter's") masking tape**, for masking

**Transfer paper, tracing paper and stylus**, for transferring pattern details

**Brush cleaner soap**, for cleaning brushes

## Surface Preparation

Be sure the jar is clean and dry before applying paint. Rub the surface with rubbing alcohol or white vinegar, holding the jar by the jar neck to avoid fingerprints. Some glass paints require an undercoat. Follow the manufacturer's instructions for best results.

## Transferring Designs

If the jar hasn't been basecoated, you can trace the pattern onto tracing paper and place it inside the jar. Secure the pattern at the top with a small piece of tape and place two or three crumpled paper towels in the jar to hold the pattern tight to the inside of the jar. (It's difficult to tape a pattern flat against the glass, but this paper towel method works well.)

When transferring a pattern to painted glass, use wax-free transfer paper. Carefully tape the transfer paper in place over the jar, making sure the paper is right side down, and tape the pattern that has been traced onto tracing paper on top. With a stylus or ball-point pen, trace over the pattern lines firmly to transfer the design to the jar.

## Basecoating

Paints can be applied to glass in a number of ways for full opaque coverage:

**Brushing:** Brush on a fairly heavy coat of paint, enough to coat the glass without dripping. Two or three coats are usually needed. Let dry fully between coats.

**Stippling:** Apply paint by pouncing with a sea sponge. Make sure the sponge is damp, not wet - squeeze out all excess water. Dip the sponge in the paint and apply to the jar in an up and down dabbing motion. You will need to apply two or three coats for full coverage and let each coat dry fully before applying another. This method gives the finished paint surface a slight texture.

## Stenciling

You can use a pre-cut, purchased stencil or cut your own from freezer paper.

1. To cut your own stencil, tape the copied pattern over a piece of freezer paper, shiny side up, that is 1" larger than the pattern.
2. Place the papers on a cutting mat and cut out the motifs, using a sharp craft knife.
3. Spray the back of the stencil with spray adhesive. Let the adhesive dry for 10 minutes, then place on the jar. (This makes your stencil adhere to the jar and allows you to remove it without tearing.)
4. Load a dense foam sponge with paint and blot on a paper towel to remove the excess. TIP: Too much paint on the sponge will cause seepage under the stencil.
5. Pounce the color over the open areas of the stencil with an up-and-down dabbing motion. It is best to use very little paint and apply several coats, if necessary. NOTE: Paint can't be swirled on slick glass surfaces.

*Positioning a traced pattern inside a jar.*

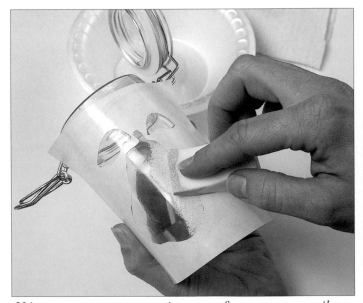

*Using a sponge to pounce paint over a freezer paper stencil.*

# Rosebud Swag Jar

See the following page for instructions.

# Floral Swag Jars

These painted jars are a romantic addition to a bath or bedroom.
Use them to store cotton swabs, make-up remover pads, or cotton balls.

## JAR TYPE

3 storage jars, 22-oz. size, with glass tops, 5-1/2" high

## SUPPLIES

Acrylic enamels for glass - White, light green, pink, purple, blue, yellow

Transparent painting medium

Artist's paint brushes - 1/2" flat, #6 flat, #4 filbert, #4 round, #1 liner

Round toothpicks

Palette

Basic Painting Supplies (See the list at the beginning of this section.)

White satin ribbon, 1/4" wide - 1 yd. per jar

3 white buttons, shanks removed

Glue

## JAR DECORATION

*See the Painting Guide on page 34.*

**Preparation:**

1. Clean the jar surfaces.
2. Trace the patterns. Place inside jars.

**Swags:**

1. Mix white paint with an equal amount of transparent medium.
2. Divide each jar into four equal sections and mark with drops of paint on the necks of the jars.
3. Using the 1/2" flat brush with the white paint mix, paint a C-stroke from one mark to the next. Wiggle the brush to get a slight scalloped edge on the swag.
4. Using the #6 flat brush, add additional folds to the swag.

5. Use a round toothpick to add dots of white paint (with NO added medium) to the bottoms of the swags and the added folds. Let dry completely.

**Lilies of the Valley:**

1. Using the #6 flat brush with light green, paint the leaves.
2. Using the liner brush with light green, add the stems. (Painting Guide, Step 1) Let dry completely.
3. Using the filbert brush with white paint, add the white flower buds. Make the flowers smaller as you work towards the end of the stem. (Painting Guide, Step 2)
4. Use a round toothpick with white paint to add two to three dots to each flower. (Painting Guide, Step 3)

**Forget-Me-Nots:**

1. Using the #6 flat brush with light green paint, paint the leaves. Using the liner brush with light green paint, paint the stems. (Painting Guide, Step 1) Let dry completely.
2. Mix blue and purple paints with white paint for paler tones. Use the round brush with the blue and purple color mixes to paint flower petals and buds. Make the flowers gradually smaller as you paint towards the end of the stem. (Painting Guide, Step 2)
3. Use a round toothpick with yellow paint to dot the center of each flower. Add a few light green dots and tiny leaves to the end of each stem. (Painting Guide, Step 3)

*Instructions continued on page 35*

*Pictured right:* Forget-Me-Not Jar, Lilies of the Valley Jar.

Floral Swag Painting Guide

Swags

Rosebuds

Lilies of the Valley

Forget-Me-Nots

# Patterns for Floral Swag Jars

### Pattern for Rosebud Swag Jar

### Pattern for Forget-Me-Nots

### Pattern for Lilies of the Valley

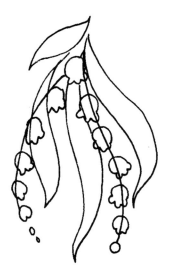

*continued from page 32*

**Rosebuds:**

1. Use the 1/2" flat brush to paint two C-strokes with pink paint to create the rosebuds. (Painting Guide, Step 1)
2. Using the round brush with light green paint, add the calyx. (painting Guide, Step 2)
3. Using the #6 flat brush with light green, paint the leaves. Finish the nosegay with thin green stems, using the liner brush. (Painting Guide, Step 3)

## LID DECORATION

Following the instructions for painting the swags, paint a lacy doily on each lid.

## EMBELLISHMENTS

Wrap the satin ribbon around the neck of each jar twice, ending with a bow. Glue a white button over the knot.

# Seasonal Jars

These easy-to-paint jars, decorated with seasonal motifs, are ready to fill for storage or gift jars. Follow the instructions at the beginning of this section for cutting and painting with stencils.

## JAR TYPE
3 wide-mouth, quart-size canning jars with metal lids and bands

## SUPPLIES
Acrylic enamels for glass - Metallic gold, metallic silver, dark green, burgundy, lime green, dark pink, medium green, yellow, white, black

Masking tape

Freezer paper, cutting mat, and craft knife

Fine sea sponge

Artist's paint brushes - #1 liner, #1 round

Round toothpick

Dense foam sponges (make-up sponges)

Palette *or* foam plate

Basic Painting Supplies (See the list at the beginning of this section.)

Coordinating fabric (for lids)

Colored raffia

Embellishments - Artificial acorn, strawberry, bumblebee; silk daisy

## JAR DECORATION
**Preparation:**
1. Tape off the bottom half of each jar with masking tape.
2. Trace the stencil patterns on freezer paper and cut out.

**Spring Strawberries:**
1. Using the sea sponge with lime green paint, sponge the bottom half of the jar. Let dry completely.
2. Using a dense foam sponge with dark pink paint, stencil the large strawberries.
3. Using the same sponge, stencil the small strawberries with dark pink paint. Shade some of the small strawberries with green paint.
4. With medium green paint, stencil the large and small leaves.
5. Using the liner brush with dark green paint, add stems and veins to the leaves.
6. Add bracts to the top of each berry with dark green paint, using the round brush.
7. Add yellow seeds to the strawberries, using the liner brush.

**Summer Bumblebees:**
1. Using the sea sponge with dark green paint, sponge the bottom half of the jar. Let dry completely.
2. Using the dense foam sponge with yellow paint, stencil the bee bodies.
3. Stencil the wings with the silver paint.
4. Using the round brush with black paint, add the black stripes and the bees' heads.
5. Using the liner brush with white paint, add details to the wings and dots for the eyes.
6. Dot the flight lines, using a round toothpick with silver paint.

**Fall Leaves:**
1. Using the sea sponge with gold metallic paint, sponge the bottom half of the jar. Let dry completely.
2. Using a dense foam sponge with green and burgundy paints, stencil the large oak leaves.
3. Using the same sponge, add gold paint to the palette and stencil the smaller leaves.

Instructions continued on page 38

*continued from page 36*

4. Using the same sponge, stencil acorns with gold paint. There should be a little green paint and burgundy paint on the sponge so the acorns show up on the gold background.
5. Stencil the acorn caps with dark green paint.
6. Using the liner brush with dark green paint, add stems to the acorns and leaves.
7. Using the liner brush with gold paint, add the veins to the leaves and details to the acorn caps.

## LID DECORATION

Cut a fabric cover for each jar. Place over the metal lids and install the bands.

## EMBELLISHMENTS

1. Wrap raffia around the bands and tie.
2. Add an artificial berry to the knot of the strawberry jar and an acorn to the leaves jar. On the bumblebee jar, add a silk daisy and artificial bee to the top of the lid. ❏

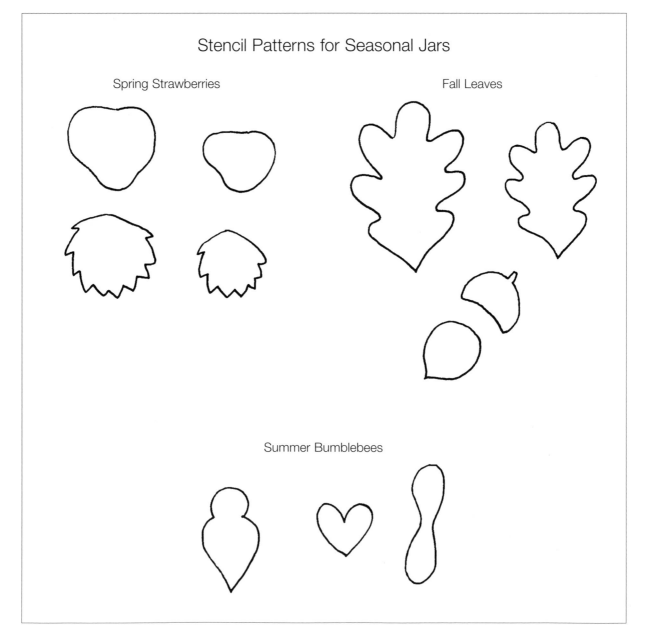

### Stencil Patterns for Seasonal Jars

Spring Strawberries

Fall Leaves

Summer Bumblebees

# Retro Storage Jars

*Instructions begin on page 42.*

# Retro Storage Jars

These stenciled jars sport retro colors and motifs reminiscent of the 1960s. The stencils are simple and very easy to cut from freezer paper; you could also use a pre-cut stencil from your local craft store. Use the jars for storage in the kitchen, bath, bedroom, or office.

*Pictured on page 40 - 41*

## JAR TYPE
3 glass storage jars with glass lids, 4-1/2" square, 28-oz.

## SUPPLIES
Acrylic enamels for glass - Turquoise, dark sage green, bright pink

Masking tape

Freezer paper, cutting mat, and craft knife *or* pre-cut stencils with dots, stripes, and rectangles

Dense foam sponges (make-up sponges)

Palette *or* foam plate

Basic Painting Supplies (See the list at the beginning of this section.)

Matching colored card paper

3 metal label holders

Strong glue for metal

## JAR DECORATION
**Preparation:**
Cut the stencils from freezer paper, using the patterns provided.

**Painting:**
Using the stencils with one paint color, stencil motifs on the sides of the jars. Let the first color dry completely before adding the additional colors. Turn the stencil upside down or stencil selected motifs to make random patterns. Repeat until the sides of the jars are decorated. Use the photo as a guide. Let dry completely.

## LID DECORATION
1. Tape off the edges of the lids with masking tape. Stencil with one color on each jar to create the colored bands. Let dry. Remove tape.
2. Stencil the tops of the lids with the same colors and motifs as the jars. Let paint dry and cure.

## EMBELLISHMENTS
1. Glue a label holder to the rim of each lid.
2. Trim the card paper to make labels. Insert in the holders. ❏

Stencil Patterns for Retro Storage Jars

# Faux Blown Glass Candle Jars

The insides of these jars have been coated with colored transparent paint to mimic
the look of blown glass - you won't believe how simple they are to create!
Each jar is topped with a decorative metal collar and embellished with a metal motif.
When the candles inside are lit, their beauty shines through.
PLEASE NOTE: Since these jars are painted on the inside, they can't be used for food.

## JAR TYPE
3 globe recycled jars, 10-oz. size

## SUPPLIES
Transparent acrylic paints for glass - Three colors (your
choice), metallic gold

Basic Painting Supplies (See the list at the beginning of this
section.)

Metal glue

Brass metal sheet, 44 gauge - one 2" x 12" strip per jar

6 gold brads (2 per jar)

Wax paper

Protective work gloves, such as leather or heavy canvas

Metal flower motifs

## TOOLS
Hole punch

Tin snips

Bone folder or wooden craft stick

Ruler

Craft knife

*Optional:* Tracing wheel

## JAR DECORATION
1. Squeeze one color of transparent paint and metallic gold
   transparent paint into the bottom of each jar and down
   the insides.
2. Turn the jars upside down on wax paper for one hour to
   drain the excess paint. After an hour, place the jars upright
   and let them dry overnight.
3. Check to be sure the entire inside of the jar is covered with
   paint. If not, add more paint and repeat step 2.
4. Add additional gold paint to the insides of the jars in thin
   streams and let run to the bottom. (This creates a nice
   striped design.) Let dry completely.
5. Use a craft knife to carefully cut away the paint from the
   inside top edge of the jar. Be careful not to peel away paint
   from the jar sides. Be sure to wear protective gloves when
   doing this.

## EMBELLISHMENTS
1. Score and fold each edge of each brass sheet piece toward
   the center creating strips 1" wide. Use a bone folder or
   wooden stick to burnish and smooth the edges. Wear protective gloves - the edges are sharp.

44

2. *Option:* Use the tracing wheel to emboss a stippled design on the top and bottom edges of each band.
3. Shape each band into a 2-1/2" diameter circle. Check to make sure each fits over the top of a jar with a little slack.
4. Punch two holes through the overlapping ends. Fasten with brass brads.
5. Place one band on each jar. Glue the bands to the tops of the jars.
6. Glue a metal flower to the front of each jar with metal glue. ❑

# DECOUPAGED JARS

With decoupage, you can decorate jars with many types of paper or with fabric. You can choose to add a few cutout motifs, cover a jar completely, or compose a collage. Lightweight decoupage paper and gift wrapping paper are the best types of paper for decoupage. I also like to use printed napkins, handmade papers, and collage papers. You can also use fabrics to cover a jar - 100% cottons and cotton-polyester blends work best. Avoid using heavy fabrics like terrycloth and fabrics with a nap, such as velvet or corduroy.

You will need two basic skills - careful cutting and gluing - to create heirloom quality projects you will be proud to display and give as gifts. Decoupage is done in three basic steps: cutting, gluing, and sealing. A "podge"-type decoupage medium can be used for both gluing and sealing.

## Supplies for Decoupage

**Paper or fabric** of your choice

**Decoupage medium**, sometimes labeled "decoupage finish"

**Sponge brush**, for applying medium

**Craft knife** and **sharp scissors**, for cutting designs

**Cutting mat**, to use with a craft knife

**Freezer paper**, to cover your work surface

*Optional:*

**Thin-bodied white glue,** as an alternative for adhering paper or fabric

**Waterbase varnish**, for sealing

**Two-part resin coating**, for a waterproof finish

NOTE: You can seal a decoupaged jar with acrylic varnish, but the jar would not be waterproof and water could ruin the decoupaged design if, for example, you used the jar as a vase. To make a decoupaged design truly waterproof and permanent, apply a two-part resin coating to the jar. See the section on Resin-Coated Jars for more information and instructions.

# The Decoupage Technique

*Here's how to apply motifs to jars:*

## Cutting

Trim away excess paper from around the image, using a craft knife and cutting mat to remove any inside areas before cutting around the outer edges with small, sharp, pointed scissors. Hold the scissors at a 45-degree angle to create a tiny beveled edge on the paper. (This edge helps the image fit snugly against the surface.) Move the print, not the scissors as you cut.

*Options:* After cutting out an image, you can decorate it further with stamping or antique the edges with an ink pad and dense foam sponge.

## Sealing

To seal the decoupaged design, apply two to three coats of decoupage medium with the foam brush. The finish appears cloudy when wet but dries crystal clear. (**photo 3**)

If you are planning to coat your project with pour-on resin, seal the decoupaged surface with thin-bodied white glue.

## Gluing

Cover your working surface with freezer paper to protect it. Use a 1" foam brush to lightly coat the back of the image with decoupage medium. (**photo 1**) Place in position on the surface and use your fingers to smooth it, pushing out wrinkles and air bubbles. (**photo 2**) Allow to dry before proceeding.

# Decoupaged Fabric-Covered Jars

Fabric-covered jars are my favorites. The fabric is cut into strips so it's easy to apply, and the jars can be embellished in a range of coordinating colors and themes. It takes 1/4 yard of fabric to cover a jar. You can use patterned fabrics and reproduce the pattern quite well if you glue the strips in order. For a different effect, you can tear the strips, creating a frayed striped look.

## Basic Supplies for Fabric-Covered Jars

**Fabric** - Cotton or cotton blend

**Cutting tools** - Scissors, rotary cutter, ruler, cutting mat

**Decoupage medium, podge-style glue, or thin-bodied white glue**, to adhere fabric

**1" flat brush**, for applying medium or glue

**Embellishments** - Cotton lace, lace appliques, fabric motifs cut from a large-patterned fabric, fabric labels

## Basic Instructions for Fabric-Covered Jars

1. Using a rotary cutter, ruler, and cutting mat, cut the fabric into strips 1" wide and 8" long. You will need about 14 strips to cover a quart size-canning jar.
2. Brush decoupage medium, podge-style glue, or thin-bodied white glue on the jar surface with a brush. Press the fabric strips over the wet glue, overlapping them slightly.
3. Cover the entire surface with a thin coating of glue.
4. Cut a 3" circle of fabric and glue on the bottom of the jar to cover the ends of the strips. Coat this end piece with a thin layer of glue as well. Let dry.
5. Glue embellishments to the jar, using the white glue. Let dry. Apply a thin coating of glue. ❏

# Decoupage Collage

Collage is a fine art technique where papers and objects are arranged and adhered to a surface. Many jars in this section are examples of collage. Use collage jars for fancy storage for on a desk or counter, as bases to hold candles, or as wonderful gift packages. The collage jars were coated with a two-part resin for a professional, finished look. (For instructions, see the section on Resin-Coated Jars.) I've included tips for creating collage jars and outlined the basic steps.

## Basic Instructions for Decoupage Collage

1. To cover a quart-size wide-mouth canning jar, cut a piece of paper 5-1/2" x 12". Cut slits with scissors, 1/2" apart, across the long top of the paper piece. (**photo 1**)
2. Apply a thin layer of decoupage medium or glue to the entire back surface of the paper. Wrap the paper around the jar, smoothing out all the bubbles and wrinkles. The cut pieces at the top will overlap slightly the curved shoulder of the jar, preventing large wrinkles. (**photo 2**)
3. Assemble a selection of stamped and printed images that work with your theme. Cut the decorative papers into strips or panels. Attach them to the jar with the decoupage medium. (**photo 3**) Let dry.

4. Decorate the flat lid to match the jar.
5. Brush the entire composition with two thin coats of thin-bodied white glue to seal the images. Let dry completely before proceeding.
6. Paint the screw-on band with acrylic enamel.
7. Apply a two-part resin coating to the jar and the flat lid. After the excess resin has dripped off the lid, place the metal band on the lid. It will adhere tightly. *Option:* If you decide not to add a resin coating, apply four to five coats of clear-drying waterbase varnish to finish your jar.
8. Glue the accent pieces to the jar. Decorate the screw-on band. ❏

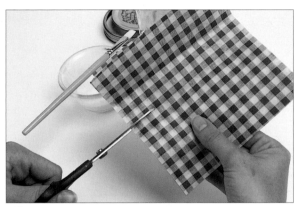

*Photo 1*

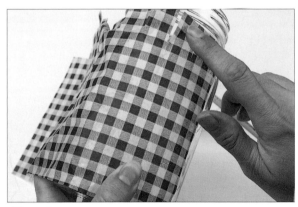

*Photo 2*

*Photo 3*

## TIPS FOR CREATING DECOUPAGE COLLAGE JARS

- Choose a theme, then work within it. A theme can be as simple as the color red, or more complicated, such as "travel to Paris." Collect images, colors, phrases, photographs, textures, and ephemera that relate to your theme.

- Consider using theme collage sheets. These papers are printed with images that make interesting additions to a collage. They enable you to use reproduced precious images from bygone eras to add beautiful images to your collages and decoupage projects. Find them, along with many beautiful collage papers, stickers, and ephemera packages, at crafts stores or stamping and scrapbooking shops.

- The background paper should cover most of the jar. Use a thin paper, such as gift wrap, tissue, thin handmade paper, or decoupage paper, rather than heavier (card weight) paper.

- Use smaller images to create the collage. (Smaller images fit nicely on curved surfaces.)

- Paper images can be ripped, torn, or cut with a straight or decorative edge. Use a variety of edges, not all straight, not all torn.

- Think about framing paper pieces with a darker piece behind them, edging the piece with ink, or using different shapes to visually break up the composition.

- Repeating a motif, color, or accent in your composition brings everything together. Variety is good, but repetition gives rhythm to a composition.

- Use clear decoupage medium or thin-bodied white glue to adhere papers to jars.

- Accents usually are objects other than paper that bring dimension to the composition. For jars, try ribbons, charms, beads, and trims - all can be used. Attach them with a glue gun and clear glue sticks.

- If you decide not to apply a resin coating, apply four to five coats of a good waterbase varnish to protect your jar.

- Above all, be creative and have fun! Don't be afraid to place items upside down, sideways, or overlapping - it's your work of art. Make it a reflection of you and your love of working with beautiful materials.

# Vintage Storage Jars

This charming canister set is decorated with vintage label stickers and metal label holders. Use them in the laundry room to hold clothespins, dryer sheets, and special-use detergents or in the office break room to hold coffee, tea, and sugar.
Instead of the stickers, you could use labels cut from decoupage paper or photocopied labels from a copyright-free image book.

## JAR TYPE
3 wide-mouth wire bail jars with glass lids

## SUPPLIES
1" sponge brush

Decoupage medium

Decorative paper with vintage advertisements

Antique label stickers or images

Metal label holders

Cream card paper

Metal glue

Garden jute - 14" per jar

Mini wooden clothespin

## JAR DECORATION
1. Cut the decorative paper into 2-1/2" x 8-1/2" strips.
2. Glue the strips to the jar with decoupage medium. Let dry.
3. Apply label stickers to jars or adhere label cutouts with decoupage medium.
4. Coat the images with one coat of decoupage medium. Let dry completely.
5. Adhere the metal label holder to the front of the jar with metal glue.
6. Cut card paper to fit the label holders.

## EMBELLISHMENTS
1. Wrap and tie a piece of garden jute around the neck of each jar.
2. Clip a mini clothespin on the jute

50

# Natural Storage Canisters

Beautiful handmade natural papers and decorative fibers are attractive embellishments for large storage jars. The lid accents and labels are made with polymer clay and painted for an antique look. In the pantry, fill them with homemade granola or crackers or use them as countertop canisters for flour and sugar.

Attaching the fibers with decoupage medium holds them in place and prevents slipping and accidental dropping of the canister during use.

## JAR TYPE
Wide-mouth wire bail glass canisters with glass lids, 8-1/2" tall

## SUPPLIES
Green and natural handmade papers, 20" x 30" sheets

Matching decorative fibers

Decoupage medium

1" flat brush

2 oz. pkg. transparent polymer clay

Ground cinnamon or other spice

Rubber stamp - Leaf motif

Acrylic craft paint - Burnt sienna

Polymer clay roller, knife

Plastic straw

Black permanent pen

## JAR DECORATION
1. Tear the handmade paper into 4" x 18" strips. Glue strips around the middle of each jar with decoupage medium. Coat the paper with an additional application of decoupage medium.
2. Tear two 3" paper circles and decoupage to the lids.
3. Wrap color-coordinated fibers around the middle of each jar, gluing with decoupage medium as you go, to make a band 1-1/2" to 2" wide. Let dry.
4. Brush the fibers with an additional coat of decoupage medium.

## EMBELLISHMENTS
1. Condition the polymer clay and mix in a teaspoon of ground cinnamon.
2. Roll the clay into thin sheets with a roller or with a pasta machine dedicated to use with polymer clay.
3. Tear four tag shapes from the clay sheets. Stack them on top of each other and roll again to compress. (This creates a rustic-looking tag with an irregular edge.) Use a plastic straw to make a hole at the top of the tag. Make a second tag.
4. Repeat the steps to make two 1-1/2" squares. Press the rubber stamp into the squares.
5. Bake the tags and square accent pieces according to the clay manufacturer's directions. Let cool.
6. Brush the tags and squares with acrylic paint. Rub off the excess paint, leaving paint along the rough edges and in the stamped motifs.
7. Use 10" strands of decorative fibers to tie the tags to the jars. Use a black permanent pen to write on the tags.
8. Glue a square accent to the top of each lid. ❑

# Sewing Collage Jar

This would make an interesting flower vase for the sewing room or a striking storage jar for sewing supplies.

## JAR TYPE
Wide-mouth quart-size canning jar

## SUPPLIES
Old tissue paper sewing pattern

Sewing theme stickers and images on paper

Basic Supplies for Resin Coating (See the section on Resin-Coated Jars.)

White glue

Buttons

12" printed trim

## TOOLS
Scissors

Glue gun and glue sticks

## JAR DECORATION
1. Cut up the tissue paper pattern and decoupage on the jar.
2. Adhere stickers, labels, and cutout images to create a collage.
3. Glue the trim around the rim of the jar.
4. Use a glue gun to attach the buttons.
5. Brush the entire composition with two thin coats of decoupage medium to seal the images. Let dry completely.
6. Coat the jar with the two-part resin following the instructions the section on Resin-Coated Jars. Be sure to cover the button trim with the resin to help permanently adhere them to the jar. ❑

# Ballet Dreams

## JAR TYPE
Wide-mouth quart-size canning jar

## SUPPLIES
Variegated pink to blue mulberry
 paper (for the background)

Ballet stickers, dream sayings, and
 decoupage images

Basic Supplies for Resin Coating (See
 the section on Resin-Coated Jars.)

White glue

Glass beads - Pink, purple, blue

Thin gold elastic cord

12" decorative fiber trim

## TOOLS
Scissors

Hot glue gun and glue sticks

## JAR DECORATION
1. Cut the mulberry paper and
 decoupage on the jar.
2. Create the collage with stickers,
 labels, and cutout images.
3. Brush the entire composition with
 two thin coats of decoupage medium
 to seal the images. Let dry completely before proceeding.
4. Coat the jar with the two-part resin,
 following the instructions in the
 Resin-Coated Jars section.

## EMBELLISHMENTS
1. Thread the beads on 14" of gold
 elastic cord. Knot to hold.
2. Using the glue gun, adhere the fiber
 trim to the neck of the jar.
3. Wrap the beaded cord around the
 rim. ❑

# Classical Jar

## JAR TYPE
Wide-mouth quart-size canning jar

## SUPPLIES
Gold printed tissue paper

Classical-theme stickers, labels, and decoupage images on paper

Basic Supplies for Resin Coating (See the section on Resin-Coated Jars.)

Decoupage medium

White glue

Gold braid trim

Thin gold cord

Polymer clay seal

Silk flowers and greenery

Gold spray paint

## JAR DECORATION
1. Cover the jar with gold tissue paper.
2. Apply stickers, labels, and cutout images to create a collage.
3. Brush the entire composition with two thin coats of decoupage medium to seal the images. Let dry completely before proceeding.
4. Coat the jar with two-part resin, following the instructions in the Resin-Coated Jars section.

## MAKING TASSELS

Fabric stores, home decor outlets, and craft stores sell a wide variety of sizes and colors of tassels. You can make plain tassels more elaborate by adding fused pearls, ribbon roses, or charms.

You can also make your own tassels by winding and gluing a lampshade fringe around the knotted end of a length of cord. Here's how:

1. Cut a 20" piece of cord and two 4" pieces of 3-1/2" lampshade fringe.
2. Fold the cord and knot the ends. Place a line of glue along the top edge of the fringe and tightly wrap around the cord ends. Let dry.
3. Embellish with fused pearl trim and a gold ribbon rose.

*Options:* Use beaded fringe, ribbon pieces, or a variety of fringe colors to make your own designer tassels. ❏

## EMBELLISHMENTS
1. Wrap the silk greenery and flowers together to make a wreath to fit over the rim of the jar.
2. Spray the wreath with a light coat of gold spray paint. Let dry.
3. Glue the wreath to the rim of the jar.
4. Cut a 20" piece of gold braid. Wrap around the neck of the jar and knot to hold. Wrap the knot with a 12" piece of thin gold cord. Separate the strands of the braid to make the tassel.
5. Glue a polymer clay seal to the top of the tassel. ❏

# Blue Buttons Jar

Tissue paper creates a translucent effect and enables you to see the contents. This jar was designed to hold buttons, but the technique can be used to create storage jars for all kinds of items, using a variety of colored and patterned tissue papers.

## JAR TYPE
Wide-mouth quart-size canning jar with plastic storage lid

## SUPPLIES
White tissue paper with navy blue dots

1" and 1-1/2" circles of turquoise tissue paper, about 12 of each

Basic Supplies for Resin Coating (See the section on Resin-Coated Jars.)

Decoupage medium

Slide mount in a matching color

1-1/2" square of white paper

White glue

20" turquoise rick rack trim

12" large navy blue rick rack trim

Blue permanent pen

Large navy blue button

Hot glue gun and glue sticks

## JAR DECORATION
1. Cover the jar with the dotted tissue paper, gluing it down with decoupage medium.
2. Glue the turquoise tissue circles in place, placed randomly on top of white tissue paper.
3. Glue a piece of turquoise rick rack around the neck of the jar.
4. Use decoupage medium to attach the white paper square where the label will be.
5. Brush the entire composition with two thin coats of decoupage medium to seal the images. Let dry completely before proceeding.
6. Glue the slide mount over the white paper square.
7. Coat the jar with two-part resin, following the instructions in the Resin-Coated Jars section.

## LID DECORATION
1. Use decoupage medium to glue the navy rick rack around the edge of the lid.
2. Glue the remaining turquoise rick rack over the navy rick rack.
3. Glue the button at the center of the lid, using a glue gun. ❏

# Natural Daisy Jar

This jar is covered with mulberry paper and pressed flowers and greenery. Coating the jar with resin makes it waterproof, so it's a perfect vase for a handful of daisies.

## JAR TYPE
Wide-mouth quart-size canning jar

## SUPPLIES
Variegated green to orange mulberry paper

Pressed daisy flowers and greenery

Basic Supplies for Resin Coating (See the section on Resin-Coated Jars.)

White glue

Paper-covered dark brown wire

## JAR DECORATION
1. Use decoupage medium to cover the jar with mulberry paper.
2. Brush the surface of the paper with decoupage medium. Position the pressed greenery and flowers on the wet medium. Let dry.
3. Using a light touch, very carefully brush on another thin coat of decoupage medium to seal the background paper and dried flowers. (The flowers are fragile and can break.) Let dry completely before proceeding.
4. Coat the jar with two-part resin coating, following the instructions in the Resin-Coated Jars section.

## EMBELLISHMENTS
Wrap the wire to form a wreath to fit around the top of the jar. It should be large enough to be easy to remove for filling and rinsing the jar. ❑

# Pink Pussycats Jar

Strips of fabric are cut and glued to the jar, band, and lid to create
a patterned collage.

## JAR TYPE

Canning jar with metal band and lid,
quart size

## SUPPLIES

Cotton cat-motif print fabric in black
and pink

Decoupage medium

1" flat brush

Pink satin ribbons

Pink decorative fibers

Silver and bead accents

Pinking shears

## JAR DECORATION

1. Cover the jar, lid, and band with
strips cut from the fabric. Let dry.
2. Cut two pieces of fabric in the shape
of a tag. Glue the pieces, wrong sides
together, with decoupage medium to
make a tag. Let dry.
3. Tie the tag and accents to the neck
of the jar with a piece of pink fiber.
4. Tie a bow with satin ribbon around
the neck of the jar. ❑

59

# Girly-girl Jars

One jar has a matching lid for storing important and secret valuables; the other, with an open top, can hold a bouquet of silk flowers or make-up brushes. They'd make great accents for a young girl's room.

## JAR TYPES

1 wide-mouth quart canning jar with metal lid and band

1 wide-mouth pint canning jar

## SUPPLIES

Bright-colored fabric in three coordinated patterns

Decoupage medium

Fabric labels

Narrow satin ribbon in matching colors

Novelty flower buttons, shanks removed

Foam flower shapes, variety of sizes*

Colored beads

Clear acetate sheet

White fabric glue

Decorative fibers in matching colors

*You can cut your own foam flower shapes from craft foam. Cut some small and some larger. On the larger shapes, cut out the center area.

## JAR DECORATION

**Large Foam Flower Accents with Center Cutout:**

1. Cut two pieces of acetate to the shape of the foam flower.
2. Stack two foam shapes with a piece of clear acetate between them. Glue together, using white fabric glue.
3. Fill the flower center with colorful beads. Glue on a clear acetate backing to the flower.

**Large Jar:**

1. Cover the jar and lid with fabric, following the instructions at the beginning of this section.
2. Adhere a fabric label and satin ribbon with decoupage medium. Let dry.
3. Glue on the flower button and foam flower accents.

**Small Jar:**

1. Cover the jar with fabric, using decoupage medium.
2. Cut out fabric motifs and adhere over the covering fabric.
3. Add satin ribbon and a fabric label, using decoupage medium. Let dry.
4. Glue on the flower button and foam flower accents.
5. Glue a large foam flower to the top of the jar.
6. Wrap and tie decorative fibers around the rim. ❏

# European Village

The plastic tags used here are recycled discontinued laminate samples from my local hardware store - usually they're free for the asking. These laminate samples can be rubber stamped, painted, and covered with paper to create unique labels for jars.

## JAR TYPE
2 canning jars with metal bands and lids

## SUPPLIES
Cotton fabric

Decoupage medium

Acrylic enamel paint to match fabric

2 yds. gold cord

2 plastic laminate "tags"

Rubber stamps and stamp pad

2 old metal keys

2 polymer clay seals

## JAR DECORATION
1. Cover the jars and the flat lids with fabric, following the instructions at the beginning of this section. Let dry.
2. Paint the metal bands with acrylic enamel.
3. Decorate the laminate tags with rubber-stamped motifs. Let dry.
4. Glue a polymer clay seal at the center of each lid.
5. Cut a 1-yd. piece of gold cord. Fold to find the center. Loop through a tag and key. Wrap the cord up and around the neck of one jar and knot in back. Repeat for other jar. ❏

# Country Pocket Jars

These fabric-covered jars sport pockets of matching fabric and lids covered with a contrasting fabric. Use the pockets to hold a recipe or instructions for a soup or cookie mix, or as a decorative touch.

## JAR TYPE
2 canning jars with plastic storage lids

## SUPPLIES
Blue denim fabric
Red gingham fabric
Decoupage medium
1" flat brush
Red rick rack trim
Cotton lace appliques
Natural jute twine
1 metal button
White fabric glue
Iron

## JAR DECORATION

**Gingham Jar:**
1. Cover the jar with gingham and the lid with denim.
2. Using the pattern provided, cut a pocket from gingham and use an iron to fold under and press the sides and top of the pocket. Use white fabric glue to hold the hems. Let dry.
3. Glue the pocket to the jar, using white fabric glue.
4. Glue red rick rack along the top of the pocket and around the edge of the lid.
5. Glue cotton lace appliques in place.
6. *Option:* Cut a pocket square from denim. Fringe or hem the edges or cut with pinking shears. Place in pocket.

**Denim Jar:**
1. Cut a piece of fabric to cover the jar. Tear the fabric in strips and to create a vertical pattern. Cover the lid with gingham.
2. Using the pattern provided, cut a pocket from denim and use an iron to fold under and press the

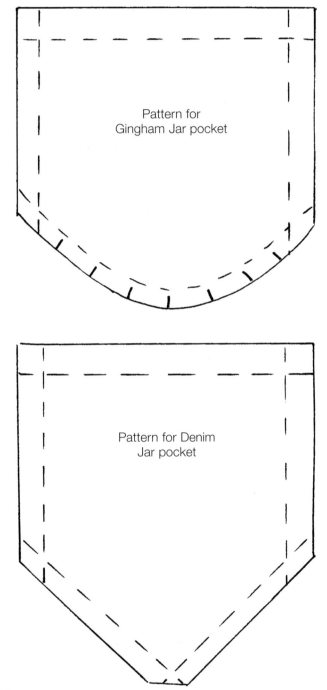

Pattern for
Gingham Jar pocket

Pattern for Denim
Jar pocket

sides and top of the pocket. Use white fabric glue to hold the hems. Let dry.

3. Glue the pocket to the jar, using white fabric glue.

4. Glue a piece of jute twine around the bottom edge of the lid.

5. Glue a metal button on the pocket.

6. *Option:* Cut a pocket square from gingham. Fringe the edges. Place in pocket. ❑

65

# Fall Harvest Jars

Celebrate the harvest with autumnal colors and motifs. Use these jars for colorful kitchen storage and to give the gifts of your garden, such as nuts, sun-dried tomatoes, or dried herbs.

## JAR TYPE
3 canning jars with metal bands and lids

## SUPPLIES
Cotton fabrics in autumn colors and patterns

Decoupage medium

1" flat brush

3 wooden tags

2 artificial acorns

Decorative fibers in autumn colors

Silk oak leaves

Gingham border stickers

Small hack saw or craft saw

Hot glue gun and glue sticks

## JAR DECORATION
1. Cover the jars, the flat lids, and the wooden tags with fabric, following the instructions at the beginning of this section.
2. Cover the metal bands with gingham border stickers.
3. Saw the artificial acorns in half. Glue a half on each tag.
4. Tie the tags around the necks of the jars with decorative fibers. ❏

66

# POLYMER CLAY
# Decorations for Jars

Polymer clay is easy to work with, comes in a wide range of colors, and bakes in your home oven. New molds make it even easier to create unique accents for jars. You can find polymer clay and tools made especially for working with it at your local crafts store.

## Basic Supplies for Polymer Clay

**Polymer clay**

**Acrylic roller** *or* a pasta machine used exclusively for polymer clay

**Plastic molding sticks**

**Polymer clay knife,** for cutting clay

**Decorative molds and stamps** for use with polymer clay

**Ceramic tile,** to use as a work surface

*Pictured right:* Polymer clay molds, molds and stamps for working with clay, and molded and stamped polymer clay decorations.

## TIPS FOR WORKING WITH POLYMER CLAY

- It is important to condition and warm the clay well before trying to mold with it. It will become more pliable and easier to work with. A pasta machine makes conditioning and rolling out clay easier and faster. It is a wise investment if you enjoy creating with this medium.
- Lightly dust the decorative molds with cornstarch to prevent the clay from sticking.
- Carefully follow the manufacturer's instructions for baking the molded objects in your oven. Be sure your room is properly ventilated during baking.
- To ensure the polymer clay pieces adhere to the slick glass surface of a jar, brush a thin coat of white glue on the back of the clay piece before placing it on the jar.
- After cooling, polymer clay can be varnished, painted, sanded, or drilled.

# Lucky Penny Office Storage

Use decorated jars on your desk to hold spare change, paper clips, and stamps. Not using the flat lids provides convenient access; a magnetic strip holds paper clips for easy use. You could also use these jars to hold pens and pencils.

*Pictured on pages 70 & 71.*

## JAR TYPES

2 standard-mouth, pint-size canning jars with metal bands

1 recycled food jar, 3-1/2" high

## SUPPLIES

Polymer clay - Black

Basic Supplies for Polymer Clay

White craft glue

Craft knife

Ruler

Metallic powders - Gold, copper, silver

Coins *or* rubber stamps of coin images

Rubber stamps with postage stamp images

Paper clips (various sizes, large and small)

Magnetic strip, 1/2" x 5"

2 yds. copper satin ribbon

3 copper pennies *or* other coins

Card paper

Decorative scissors with stamp edge

## JAR DECORATION

**Coin Jar:**

1. Roll out a thin sheet of conditioned black polymer clay.
2. Rub a coin or a coin motif rubber stamp with metallic powder and press into the clay to make an image.
3. Trim around the clay "coin" with the craft knife and remove from the sheet.
4. Glue the clay coin to the jar surface with the white glue.
5. Repeat steps 2 through 4 to create a band of clay "coins" around the jar, using both sides of a real coin to make impressions and a variety of metallic powder colors.
6. Cut a 1" x 11" strip of clay. Glue and form it around the rim and top edge of the metal band.
7. Using the edge of a wooden craft stick, impress a design into the clay around the rim.
8. Using your finger, coat the band with gold metallic powder.
9. Bake the jar band and jar in the oven following the polymer clay manufacturer's instructions.

*Continued on next page*

## Lucky Penny Office Storage
*continued from page 69*

10. Cut a 24" piece of copper satin ribbon. Loop around the jar and glue a penny to hold it in place.

**Stamp Jar:**
1. Roll out a thin sheet of conditioned black polymer clay.
2. Rub a postage stamp motif rubber stamp with metallic powder and press in the clay to make an image.
3. Trim around the "stamp" with a craft knife and cut out.
4. Glue the stamp motif to the jar with white glue.
5. Repeat steps 2 through 4 to make more "stamps." Use a variety of metallic powder colors to create a band of stamps around the jar.
6. Cut a 1" x 11" strip of clay. Glue and form it around the rim and top edge of the metal band.
7. Cut a piece of card paper with stamp-edge decorative scissors. Press it in the clay around the rim.
8. With the card paper band in place, use your finger to coat the clay band on the rim with gold metallic powder. Remove the card paper band to reveal the design.
9. Bake the band and jar in the oven, following the polymer clay manufacturer's instructions.
10. Cut a 24" piece of copper satin ribbon. Loop around the jar and glue a penny to hold it in place.

**Paper Clip Jar:**
1. Roll out a thin sheet of conditioned black polymer clay.
2. Measure the jar. Trim the polymer clay sheet to fit, using the craft knife and a ruler.
3. Press large and small paper clips into the clay to create a deep pattern.
4. Cut a 1/2" x 8" strip of polymer clay. Glue and form around the rim of the jar.
5. With your finger, coat the polymer clay band with gold and copper metallic powders.
6. Bake the jar in the oven, following the polymer clay manufacturer's instructions.
7. Glue the magnetic strip inside the rim of the jar.
8. Loop the remaining 24" piece of copper satin ribbon around the jar and glue a penny to hold in place.
9. Fill the jar with paper clips. To have paper clips at the top of the jar ready to use, shake the jar. The clips will cling to the magnetic strip. ❑

# Faux Majolica Jars

This set of jars mimics the look of majolica ceramics. They are produced in a similar fashion - by pushing soft clay into a mold and applying the molded clay to the vessel's surface. This is a good project for using up leftover bits and pieces of various colors of polymer clay.

PLEASE NOTE: Since these jars are painted on the inside, they can't be used for food.

## JAR TYPE

3 apothecary jars with glass lids, 10-oz. size, 5" high

## SUPPLIES

Polymer clay - Variety of colors

Basic Supplies for Polymer Clay

Acrylic enamel paints - Dark blue, dark purple, ochre

1/2" flat brush

White glue

Polymer clay molds - Floral motifs

Polymer clay varnish - gloss

## JAR DECORATION

1. Press conditioned polymer clay into the molds to make the floral accents.
2. Position and glue the pieces on the jars and lids with white glue, using the photo as a guide.
3. Using the pattern provided, cut out leaf shapes from a thin sheet of green polymer clay. Glue in place on a jar.
4. Bake the jars and lids in your home oven, following the clay manufacturer's instructions.
5. When the jars are completely cool, paint the insides of the jars and lids with acrylic enamel paints. Let dry.
6. Apply a coat of gloss varnish to the polymer clay motifs for a shiny finish. ❏

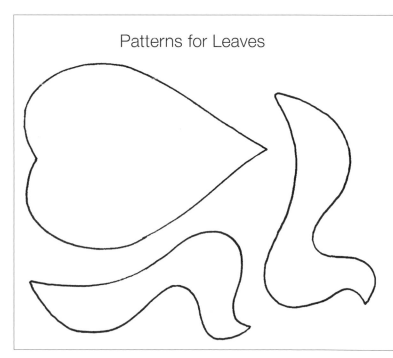

Patterns for Leaves

# MOSAIC JARS

Mosaic jars are pleasing and rewarding to create. The projects in this section are made with pre-cut glass and mirror tiles and flat marbles to make functional containers that will last many years.

## Basic Supplies for Mosaics

**Glass mosaic tiles and flat marbles** in a variety of sizes and colors

**Glass tile adhesive**, for gluing

**Glue brush**

**Colored grout**, for filling the spaces between the tiles

**Grout applicator spatula**

**Float sponge** - a specially designed sponge for smoothing and removing the excess grout

**Plastic mixing tub** for mixing grout

**Masking tape** for holding tiles in place until the adhesive dries

**Bucket**, to hold water for rinsing

*Basic Instructions on pages 76 and 77.*

# Basic Mosaic Instructions

## Basic Mosaic Instructions

1. Working one section at a time, with the jar propped on its side, apply the tile adhesive to the jar with a glue brush. **(photo 1)**

2. Position the tiles on the jar with small spaces between them. **(photo 2)** Let the adhesive dry before going on to the next section. TIP: Use tape to secure larger, heavier tiles and marbles to the jar to prevent them from slipping off the rounded surface while the adhesive dries.

3. Glue the remaining tiles to the surface, working in small sections. Let dry completely before proceeding.

4. Mix the grout according to the package instructions - you need approximately 1/4 cup of mixed grout for a pint jar. The mixed grout should be the consistency of very thick cream.

5. Apply the grout using the flat edge spatula, filling all the spaces between the tiles. **(photo 3)**

6. Smooth the grout along the top and bottom edges of the jar with your fingers to give an even, finished look. Be careful - tiles can be sharp!

7. Let the grout set up for about 20 minutes, then clean the tile surface with the rubber edge of the float sponge. **(photo 4)** Rinse the sponge often in clean water and repeat to remove the grout from the tiles. Use a large bucket with water to rinse the sponge. Never pour the rinsing water down a drain.

8. Let the grout dry. Periodically wipe the mosaic with a damp sponge to remove the film that accumulates.

9. *Option:* Rub the dry tiles with olive oil for extra sheen. ❏

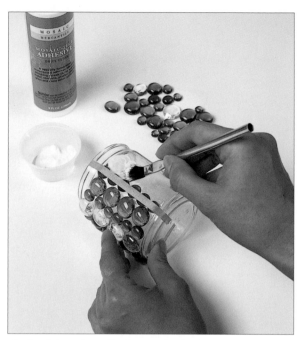

*1. Applying the adhesive to the jar.*

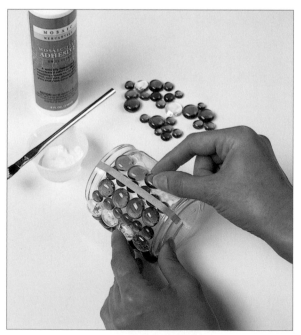

*2. Positioning the tiles on the adhesive.*

*3. Grouting the design.*

*4. Removing excess grout with a wet sponge.*

# Mirror
# Mosaic Box

Mosaics on jars make gorgeous tabletop accents. Here, a square jar was covered with mirror tiles and clear glass marbles to create a mosaic box. It looks especially nice surrounded by candles - the mirrors reflect the flickering light.

## JAR TYPE
Square glass storage canister, 28-oz. size,
   4-1/2" square

## SUPPLIES
Mirror tiles, plain and embossed, 1/2" square
   (You'll need about 180 in all.)

Clear flat-back marbles, 1/4"
   (You'll need 60-70 pieces.)

Basic Supplies for Mosaics

Black grout

## JAR DECORATION
*See the Basic Mosaic Instructions at the beginning of this section.*
1. Cover the jar with mirror tiles, using the photo as a guide for placement. Attach clear marbles along the corners and on the edge of the lid.
2. Apply the grout. Let dry thoroughly. ❑

# Mosaic Lights

These jar lights are perfect for hanging outdoors to light a summer's eve.
The candlelight shines through the colored glass pieces, making the lanterns glow.
I used color-coordinated packages of glass pieces from a crafts store.
The top loop of the wire hanger should be at least 8" above the jar to prevent
overheating from the candle flame.

*Pictured opposite and on the following pages.*

## JAR TYPE
1/2 pint-size canning jars

## SUPPLIES
Basic Supplies for Mosaics

Glass shards, half marbles and mirror tiles,
50-60 pieces per jar

Ivory grout

20 gauge aluminum sheet - You need a 2" x 12"
strip for each jar.

18 gauge aluminum armature wire - You need 36"
for each jar.

Silver paper brads - 2 per jar

Masking tape

Wooden craft stick

1/8" hole punch

Metal glue

Tin snips to cut the metal sheet

Protective work gloves, such as leather or canvas

## JAR DECORATION
*See the Basic Mosaic Instructions at the beginning of
this section.*
1. Following the basic instructions, cover the jars
   below the rims with colored glass pieces in a
   random design.
2. Apply the grout. Let the jars dry thoroughly.

## EMBELLISHMENTS
**Metal Bands:**
*Make one band for each jar.*
1. Score and fold in each long edge of the
   aluminum strips to create a strip 1" wide. Using
   a wooden craft stick, burnish the edges to flatten
   them. Wear protective gloves - the edges are sharp!
2. Shape the band to make a 3-1/2" diameter circle
   - it should fit around the top of the jar with a
   little slack.
3. Complete the band by punching two holes
   through the overlapping ends. Fasten with silver
   brads. Set aside.

**Wire Hangers:**
*Make one for each jar.*
1. Cut two pieces of wire, one 12" and one 24".
2. Fold the 24" wire in half and twist the top to
   form a loop for hanging. Curl both ends.
3. Tape the ends of the wire hanger to the rim of
   the jar to hold them in place. Wrap the 12"
   piece of wire around the rim to hold the hanger
   in place. Twist, trim, and fold down the sharp
   ends. Remove the tape.

**Assembly:**
1. Slip the metal band around the top of the jar
   and press to hold the hanger firmly in place.
2. Use strong metal glue to secure the band firmly
   to the jar. ❏

*Pictured at right:* Marble Mosaic Jar. This mosaic is
made entirely with flat-backed marbles of different
sizes. I accented the collar with additional silver brads.

# Mosaic Lights

*Instructions begin on page 78.*

# CHARACTER JARS

These cute, colorful tops were designed for jars that hold favorite layered mixes
or treats. They are surprisingly simple to make and a perfect project for older children
to help with. The supplies are inexpensive and easy to find.
The basic construction is the same for all the designs; different patterns and colors
create the different characters. I used recycled jars with colored plastic lids,
but the patterns would easily fit standard pint canning jars.

## Basic Supplies for Character Jars

**Plastic foam ball**, 3", for the character heads

**Felt**, for the decorations

**Adhesives** - Hot glue gun and clear glue sticks,
white fabric glue

**Embellishments** - Plastic eyes, 1/4"; pins with
round colored heads; colored chalks; raffia,
trim, or decorative fibers

**Tools** - Serrated knife (for cutting plastic foam),
scissors, stiff paint brush (for applying chalk)

**Wax paper**, to protect your work surface

**Paint pens**, for writing on jars

## Basic Instructions for Character Jars

1. Cut the foam ball in half, using a serrated
knife.
2. Cut a circle of felt 6" in diameter in the base
color for your character.
3. Using the patterns provided, cut the remaining
pieces of felt in the colors indicated on the
patterns.
4. Place the foam ball, flat side down, on a piece of
wax paper. Coat the foam ball with fabric glue.

5. Center and place the felt circle over the foam
ball half and pull the felt over the ball, stretching
the felt slightly to remove any creases. Hold the
felt to the ball until it adheres. Let dry
completely.
6. Trim the excess felt 1/2" from the bottom edge
of the foam ball half. Using scissors, clip a
fringe from the overhanging felt. Set aside.
7. Using the glue gun, center and glue the large
felt pieces to the top of the lid in order.
8. Using the glue gun, glue the felt-covered ball to
the center of the lid.
9. Glue the character's features and other embellishments to the covered base.
10. Highlight the character's facial features with
chalks and a stiff, clean paint brush. Use the
photo as a guide.
11. Write a fun saying or greeting on the jar with a
paint pen.
12. Tie raffia or trims around the neck of the jar
and glue on embellishments. ❏

*Pictured right:* Goofy Goblin. See the next page for
instructions.

# Goofy Goblin Jar

Fill with gummy worms, black licorice, or Sugar & Spice Nuts.

## JAR TYPE
Recycled jar with plastic lid, 5" high

## SUPPLIES
Felt - Tan, dark green, moss green

3" plastic foam ball

Serrated knife

Hot glue gun and clear glue sticks

White fabric glue

Plastic eyes, 1/4"

Pins with round colored heads

Colored chalks

Wax paper

Scissors

Raffia, trim, or decorative fibers

Stiff paint brush

Embellishments - Plastic toy bugs, black raffia

Paint pen - Black

## INSTRUCTIONS
1. Cut the foam ball in half, using a serrated knife.
2. Cut a circle of tan felt 6" in diameter.
3. Using the patterns provided, cut the remaining pieces from dark green and moss green felt.
4. Place the foam ball, flat side down, on a piece of wax paper. Coat the foam ball with fabric glue.
5. Center and place the felt circle over the foam ball half, and pull the felt over the ball, stretching the felt slightly to remove any creases. Hold the felt to the ball until it adheres. Let dry completely.
6. Trim the excess felt 1/2" from the bottom edge of the foam ball half. Using scissors, clip a fringe from the overhanging felt. Set aside.
7. Using the glue gun, center and glue the green felt pieces to the top of the lid in order.
8. Using the glue gun, glue the felt-covered ball to the center of the lid.
9. Use your thumbnail to create an impression for the mouth. Glue the character's features to the covered base.
10. Highlight the character's facial features with chalks, using a stiff, clean paint brush. Use the photo as a guide.
11. Write a fun saying or greeting (e.g., "BOO TO YOU!" or "NO TRICKS...ONLY TREATS!") on

the jar with a black paint pen.
12. Tie raffia around the neck of the jar. Glue on the toy bugs. ❑

# Patterns for Goofy Goblin Jar

Cut 1 each from tan felt

Cut 1 from moss green felt

Cut 1 from dark green felt

# Hungry Turkey Jar

Fill with Chicken Noodle Soup Mix, candy corn, or popcorn kernels.

## JAR TYPE
Recycled jar with plastic lid,
5" high

## SUPPLIES
Felt - Tan, red, brown, yellow

3" plastic foam ball

Serrated knife

Hot glue gun and clear glue sticks

White fabric glue

Plastic eyes, 1/4"

Pins with round colored heads

Colored chalks

Wax paper

Scissors

Red raffia

Stiff paint brush

Embellishments - Leaf novelty
buttons (shanks removed)

Paint pen - Red

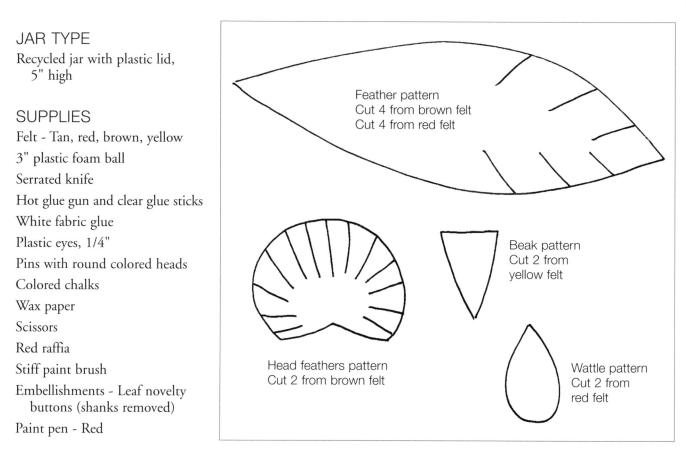

Feather pattern
Cut 4 from brown felt
Cut 4 from red felt

Beak pattern
Cut 2 from
yellow felt

Head feathers pattern
Cut 2 from brown felt

Wattle pattern
Cut 2 from
red felt

## INSTRUCTIONS
1. Cut the foam ball in half, using a serrated knife.
2. Cut a circle of tan felt 6" in diameter.
3. Using the patterns provided, cut the remaining pieces of felt from the colors indicated on the patterns.
4. Place the foam ball, flat side down, on a piece of wax paper. Coat the foam ball with fabric glue.
5. Center and place the felt circle over the foam ball half and pull the felt over the ball, stretching the felt slightly to remove any creases. Hold the felt to the ball until it adheres. Let dry completely.
6. Trim the excess felt 1/2" from the bottom edge of the foam ball half. Using scissors, clip a fringe from the overhanging felt. Set aside.
7. Using the glue gun, center and glue the feather pieces to the top of the lid.
8. Using the glue gun, glue the felt-covered ball to the center of the lid.
9. Glue the wattle, beak, head feathers, and character's features to the covered base.
10. Highlight the character's facial features with chalks, using a stiff, clean paint brush. Use the photo as a guide.
11. Write a fun saying or greeting (e.g., "GOBBLE-GOBBLE-GOBBLE!" or "HOME FOR THE HARVEST") on the jar with a red paint pen.
12. Tie red raffia around the neck of the jar and glue on the novelty buttons. ❏

# Sunny Flower Jar

Fill with jelly beans, Sugar & Spice Nuts, or a wildflower seed mix.

## JAR TYPE
Recycled jar with colored plastic lid, 5" high

## SUPPLIES
Felt - Yellow, pink, dark pink, green, lime green

3" plastic foam ball

Serrated knife

Hot glue gun and clear glue sticks

White fabric glue

Plastic eyes, 1/4"

Pins with round colored heads

Colored chalks

Wax paper

Scissors

Raffia - Gold

Stiff paint brush

Embellishments - Doll's sunglasses, ladybug buttons (shanks removed)

Paint pen - Pink

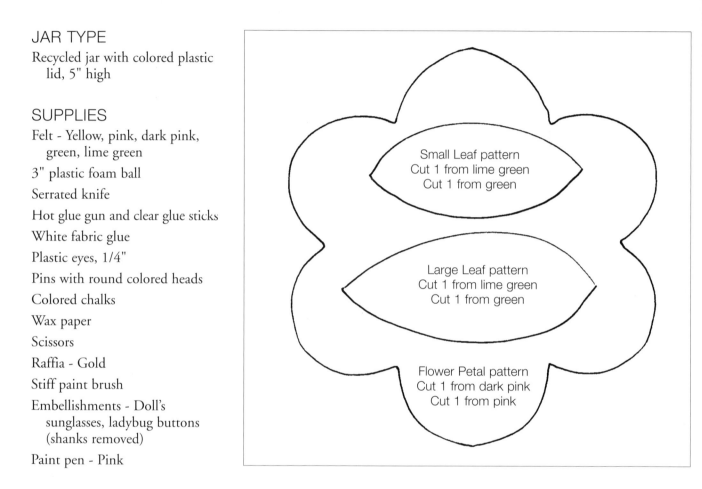

Small Leaf pattern
Cut 1 from lime green
Cut 1 from green

Large Leaf pattern
Cut 1 from lime green
Cut 1 from green

Flower Petal pattern
Cut 1 from dark pink
Cut 1 from pink

## INSTRUCTIONS

1. Cut the foam ball in half, using a serrated knife.
2. Cut a circle of yellow felt 6" in diameter.
3. Using the patterns provided, cut the remaining pieces of felt from the colors indicated on the patterns.
4. Place the foam ball, flat side down, on a piece of wax paper. Coat the foam ball with fabric glue.
5. Center and place the felt circle over the foam ball half and pull the felt over the ball, stretching the felt slightly to remove any creases. Hold the felt to the ball until it adheres. Let dry completely.
6. Trim the excess felt 1/2" from the bottom edge of the foam ball half. Using scissors, clip a fringe from the overhanging felt.
7. Using the glue gun, center and glue the leaf and flower petal pieces to the top of the lid.
8. Using the glue gun, glue the felt-covered ball to the center of the lid.
9. Glue sunglasses to the covered base.
10. Highlight the character's facial features with chalks, using a stiff, clean paint brush. Use the photo as a guide.
11. Write a fun saying or greeting (e.g., "WISHING YOU SUNSHINE" or "SUMMER BLOSSOMS") on the jar with a pink paint pen.
12. Tie gold raffia around the neck of the jar and glue on the ladybug buttons. ❑

# Sparkly Snowflake Jar

Fill with Hot Chocolate Mix, mini marshmallows, and white peppermints.

## JAR TYPE
Recycled jar with colored plastic lid, 5" high

## SUPPLIES
Felt - White, dark blue

3" plastic foam ball

Serrated knife

Hot glue gun and clear glue sticks

White fabric glue

Plastic eyes, 1/4"

Pins with round colored heads

Colored chalks

Wax paper

Scissors

Silver rick rack trim

Stiff paint brush

Embellishments - Plastic snowflakes, white wool yarn

Paint pen - White

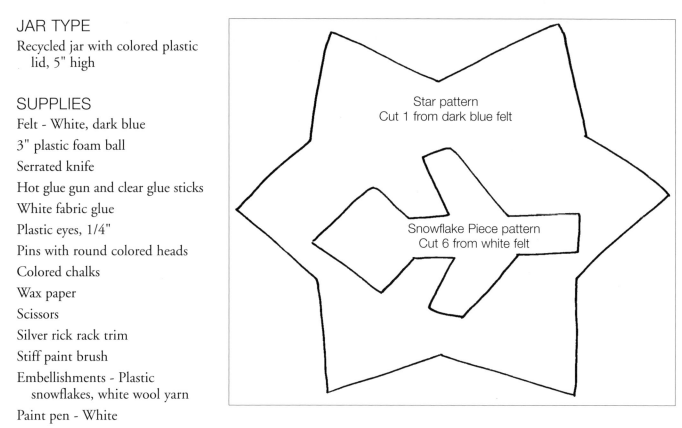

Star pattern
Cut 1 from dark blue felt

Snowflake Piece pattern
Cut 6 from white felt

## INSTRUCTIONS
1. Cut the foam ball in half, using a serrated knife.
2. Cut a circle of white felt 6" in diameter.
3. Using the patterns provided, cut the remaining pieces from white and dark blue felt as indicated on the patterns.
4. Place the foam ball, flat side down, on a piece of wax paper. Coat the foam ball with fabric glue.
5. Center and place the felt circle over the foam ball half and pull the felt over the ball, stretching the felt slightly to remove any creases. Hold the felt to the ball until it adheres. Let dry completely.
6. Trim the excess felt 1/2" from the bottom edge of the foam ball half. Using scissors, clip a fringe from the overhanging felt. Set aside.
7. Using the glue gun, center and glue the star and snowflake pieces of felt to the top of the lid.
8. Using the glue gun, glue the felt-covered ball to the center of the lid.
9. Use your thumbnail to create an impression for the mouth. Glue on the eyes and facial embellishments, using the photo as a guide.
10. Highlight the character's facial features with chalks, using a stiff, clean paint brush. Use the photo as a guide.
11. Write a fun saying or greeting (e.g., "ALL MY FRIENDS ARE FLAKES" or "FROSTY FRIENDS") on the jar with a white paint pen.
12. Tie rick rack and white yarn around the neck of the jar. Glue a snowflake over the knot of yarn and rickrack. ❑

# Pincushion Jar

I used a decorative apothecary jar for this design, but a small wide-mouth canning jar would also work nicely. It's not a character, but the Character Jar techniques are used for the domed lid - half a plastic foam ball makes a perfectly shaped cushion for the top. Use the jar to hold spools of thread, buttons, or other sewing essentials.

## JAR TYPE
Apothecary jar with flat glass lid, 3" high

## SUPPLIES
3" plastic foam ball

Cream colored fabric

Serrated knife

Fabric glue

4" white crocheted doily

Polyester batting

Buttons and sewing-themed charms

Decorative pins

12" champagne colored braid trim

12" cream printed ribbon

Wax paper

Gold-topped straight pins and hat pins

Glass beads

Jewelry glue

## LID DECORATION
1. Cut the foam ball in half, using a serrated knife.
2. Cut a circle of fabric 6" in diameter. Cut a piece of polyester batting the same size.
3. Place the foam ball, cut side down, on a piece of wax paper. Coat the foam ball with the fabric glue.
4. Cover the curved side of the ball with the batting circle. Place the fabric circle over the batting and stretch it slightly to remove any creases.
5. Trim off the excess fabric 1" from the bottom edge of the ball. Fold the remaining fabric under the foam ball. Glue to adhere.
6. Using the glue gun, center and glue the doily on the top of the lid.
7. Using the glue gun, glue the fabric covered ball on the lid, centering it.
8. Using the glue gun, adhere the braid trim around the base of the ball. Glue buttons and charms to cover the seam. Glue the cream printed ribbon around the neck of the jar.
9. To create the decorative pins, use jewelry glue to adhere glass beads to the ends of gold-topped pins. Decorate hat pins using the same technique, adding a charm to the top loop. ❑

# RESIN-COATED JARS

Using a two-part resin coating, you can make professional-looking jars and lids. The pour-on resin coating gives a hard, waterproof finish with the depth and luster equal to 50 coats of varnish, and the finished jars are practical and easy to clean.

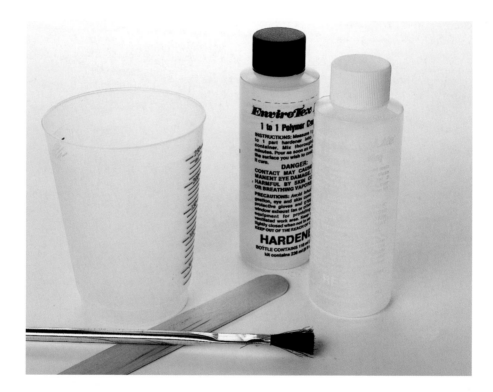

## Basic Supplies for Resin Coating

**Two-part pour-on resin coating.** The coating comes in two parts, the resin and the hardener.

**Mixing supplies:** a plastic mixing cup with accurate measurement marks, a wooden stir stick, and a disposable glue brush (These items will be discarded after use.)

**Freezer paper or wax paper,** to protect your work surface

**Disposable plastic or waxed paper cups,** to prop up your project and keep it off the work surface

**Thin-bodied white glue,** for sealing

**Clear cellophane tape** or **rubber cement,** for masking surfaces

**Fine sandpaper,** for removing drips after drying

## Applying the Coating

1. Protect the bottom of the jar with rubber cement or cellophane tape.

2. Seal all decorative treatments (paper and all porous materials, such as food items) with a coat of thin-bodied white glue that dries clear. While it is drying, place the jar right side up on a waxed paper cup to lift it away from your work surface.

3. When the glue is dry, you are ready to mix the resin. Mix only as much as you can use on your project - leftover coating cannot be saved for other projects. Measure out the two parts in the same container. You want to mix exactly 1 part resin with 1 part hardener. (**photo 1**)

4. Stir the resin and hardener with the wooden stick until thoroughly blended - this takes a full two minutes of vigorous mixing. The importance of thorough mixing cannot be over-emphasized, as poor mixing can result in a soft finish because the coating will not harden properly. Do not be concerned if bubbles get whipped into the mixture. Bubbles will be removed after the resin is poured.

5. As soon as the coating is mixed, pour it over the outside of your jar or lid. (**photo 2**) Allow the excess to drip off onto a protected surface.

6. Spread the coating, using a brush, as necessary. You have about 20 minutes to work on your project before the coating starts to set up.

7. After 5 to 10 minutes, the air bubbles created when mixing will rise to the surface. They can be easily and effectively broken by gently exhaling on them until they disappear. (The carbon dioxide in your breath breaks the bubbles.) **Avoid inhaling fumes** as you de-gas the bubbles.

8. Discard the mixing cup, the stir stick, and the brush. Allow your project to cure for a full 72 hours to a hard, permanent finish. Remove the tape or rubber cement from the bottom of the jar. Sand off excess or drips with fine sandpaper. ❑

*Photo 1 - Pouring the hardener into a measuring cup for mixing.*

### TIPS & CONSIDERATIONS

- Your work surface should be level and the area warm and free of dust.

- Your project surface should be dry and free of any dust or grease.

- The coating will drip off the sides of the project. You can protect the underside by brushing on rubber cement or covering the bottom edges with clear cellophane tape.

- Drips on unprotected surfaces can be sanded off when the finish has cured.

*Photo 2 - Pouring the coating on a lid.*

# Bean Soup Jar

This jar is topped with a scoop of colorful beans so it's perfect for storing dried beans or to give as a gift filled with a bean soup mix. I found the miniature bottle of hot sauce for sale on the company's web site - it makes a cute addition when giving the jar as a gift.

## JAR TYPE

Storage jar with red plastic lid, 6-1/2" tall.
(A quart-size wide-mouth canning jar with a plastic storage lid would also work for this project.)

## SUPPLIES

Decorative paper

Small wooden scoop

Dried beans

Basic Supplies for Resin Coating (See the beginning of this section.)

Black jute

*Optional:* Mini bottle of hot sauce

## LID DECORATION

1. Measure and cut a circle of decorative paper to fit the top of the lid. Glue the paper to the lid with white glue.
2. Coat the paper with a thin layer of white glue. Let dry until crystal clear.
3. With white glue, glue the wooden scoop and beans in place, using the photo as a guide. Let dry completely.
4. Following the instructions at the beginning of this section, apply the two-part resin coating, pouring the coating over the top of the lid. Let the resin cure. Sand off any drips.
5. Tie a piece of black jute around the neck of the jar.
6. *Option:* Use a piece of jute to tie on the bottle of hot sauce. ❏

# Game Pieces Jar

Here's a perfect storage jar to hold all those small playing pieces
that are so easily lost in the game cupboard!
Keep it for your family room or fill with game pieces and give as a gift.
I used lettered pieces to spell out "PLAY GAMES" as part of
the design. Crafts and scrapbooking stores sell game pieces
as embellishments.

## JAR TYPE

Storage jar with red plastic lid, 6-1/2" tall.
(A quart-size wide-mouth canning jar with
a plastic storage lid would also work for this
project.)

## SUPPLIES

Small playing cards

Game pieces (dominos, dice, marbles, letter tiles)

Basic Supplies for Resin Coating (See the
beginning of this section.)

## LID DECORATION

1. Glue three or four small playing cards on the top
   of the lid in a fan arrangement with the white
   glue.
2. Coat the cards with a thin layer of white glue.
   Let dry until crystal clear.
3. With white glue, glue the game pieces in place.
   Let dry completely.
4. Following the instructions at the beginning of
   this section, apply the two-part resin coating to
   the lid. Let the resin cure. Sand off any drips. ❏

# Creative Materials Jar

Use this jar to hold crayons or other creative materials so they're always ready for young artistic hands.

## JAR TYPE

Storage jar with red plastic lid, 6-1/2" tall.
(A quart-size wide-mouth canning jar with a plastic storage lid would also work for this project.)

## SUPPLIES

Colored card paper cut into 1-1/2" x 2" pieces

Novelty plastic buttons, shanks removed - Crayons, scissors, other creative supplies

Basic Supplies for Resin Coating (See the beginning of this section.)

## LID DECORATION

1. Glue the colored paper pieces on the top in a fan arrangement with white glue.
2. Coat the paper with a thin layer of the white glue. Let dry until crystal clear.
3. With white glue, glue the plastic novelty button shapes to the lid. Let dry completely.
4. Following the instructions at the beginning of this section, coat the top of the lid with resin coating. Let the resin cure. Sand off any drips. ❏

# MEMORY JARS

These memory jars contain a decorated page that's a one-page scrapbook preserved under glass. The page features a photograph and is decorated with scrapbooking supplies.
I used quart-size standard canning jars to make the Memory Jars. With the addition of a votive holder, the jar can be used as a candle holder; another option would be to add a fancy lid and place additional memorabilia inside.

## Basic Supplies for Memory Jars

**Photographs** or other memorabilia

**Scrapbooking paper**, 12" x 12". Choose a paper that complements your theme.

**Scrapbook adhesives** - glue stick, paper glue

**Embellishments** - Ribbons, fibers, stickers, and accents that coordinate with your theme

**Writing supplies**, such as pens and markers, for adding lettering

*Optional:* **Tissue paper**, to hold the page in place in the jar

## Basic Instructions for Memory Jars

1. Choose the photograph(s) you would like to use. From the photographs you've chosen, determine the theme for your jar.
2. Cut a background 5" x 12" from the 12" x 12" sheet of scrapbooking paper. This paper is your "page."
3. On the page, arrange cropped and/or framed photos, stickers, and other accents. Determine where and what type of lettering you'd like to add. Keep the focal point of the design - usually a photograph - in the center of the paper so it is central to the composition. When you are satisfied with the page design, use glue to adhere all the pieces. Add any lettering. Let dry.
4. Roll the page carefully and drop it into the jar. *Option:* Add crumpled tissue paper to the jar to help hold the decorated page in place.
5. Decorate your memory jar with ribbon, fibers, buttons, and other scrapbooking embellishments that work with your theme. ❏

# Sports Fan Memory Jar

A sports photograph and the colors black, green, and white were chosen for this candle holder jar. Use it as a tabletop accent in the family room or as part of a centerpiece for a celebration.

## JAR TYPE
Quart-size standard canning jar

## SUPPLIES
Sports photo

Sports theme stickers and accents, or collected memorabilia

Green paper

Decorative fibers

Scissors

Paper adhesives

Green glass candle holder

Black plastic numbers

Green votive candle

Adhesive for numbers if yours aren't self-adhesive

## JAR DECORATION
1. Following the instructions at the beginning of this section, make a decorated page on the green paper. Place inside the jar.
2. Attach other accents or memorabilia the outside of the jar.
3. Tie the decorative fibers around the top of the jar neck.
4. Cut a strip of the same green paper and wrap around the neck of the jar to hide the threaded top.
5. Glue the black numbers to the green glass candle holder.
6. Place in the candle holder in the jar. Place the candle in the holder. ❏

### LIGHTED JAR GIFTS

Jars are an excellent base for a candle or lamp. Check out your local craft outlet for lid lamp kits, which consist of a glass vial that fits in the lid and a funnel for pouring lamp oil in the vial. The wick burns brightly, and you can safely fill the jar with decorative objects.

Votive candles and glass votive holders also fit nicely in the tops of quart-size canning jars, creating another candle base. Fill the jars with a layered potpourri or decorative items.

**Always** provide instructions for using your lighted jar gift and remind the recipient to **never** leave a burning candle unattended.

# Sisters Memory Jar

A photograph of two girls and a sisters theme was used for this lamp jar.
The pink and black color scheme coordinates with the photo.
It's a wonderful gift for sisters to share and display or to give as
a gift to commemorate a special friendship.

## JAR TYPE
Quart-size standard canning jar

## SUPPLIES
Photograph

Papers - Pink, black and white checked

Stickers - Letters, border

Matching tag

Rub-on letters

Mini bottle cap letters to spell SISTERS

Ribbons - Black dotted, black and white checked with wire edge

Scissors

Paper adhesives

Hole punch

Lamp lid kit

## JAR DECORATION
1. Following the instructions at the beginning of this section, mount the photograph on pink paper and decorate the area around the photo with letter stickers. Place inside the jar.
2. Make a tag from checked paper and add rub-on letters and border stickers.
3. Decorate the outside of the jar with bottle cap letters that spell "SISTERS."
4. Glue a strip of checked ribbon around the rim of the lid. Use another piece of checked ribbon to attach the tag.
5. Tie the black dotted ribbon around the neck of the jar and finish with a large bow.
6. Use a lid lamp kit for the top. ❏

# Graduation Jar

Graduation photographs were chosen for this candle holder that makes a great party centerpiece and keepsake. Royal blue, the color of the graduation robe, was chosen for the paper and ribbon.

## JAR TYPE
Standard quart-size canning jar

## SUPPLIES
Photograph

Papers - Royal blue

Rub-on letters and accents with inspirational themes (e.g., "dream," "good luck")

Ribbon - Royal blue

Decorative fibers

Star buttons

Scissors

Paper adhesives

Blue glass votive holder

Blue candle

## JAR DECORATION
1. Following the instructions at the beginning of this section, make a decorated page on the blue paper. Place inside the jar.
2. Tie the decorative fibers around the top of the jar neck.
3. Tie the blue ribbon in a bow around the jar neck. Glue on star buttons over the knot to decorate.
4. Place the candle holder in the jar. Place the candle in the holder. ❑

# HOMEMADE CULINARY MIXES & RECIPES

This section includes some favorite recipes for layered jar mixes and homemade goodies to fill your decorated jars. Each mix recipe in this section comes with instructions to package with the mix.
Jars that hold food should be cleaned and sterilized before filling and should never be painted or decorated on the inside.

## Making Recipe Cards & Labels

When taking the time to create a decorated jar of layered cookie or soup mix, make sure you give the same attention to the instructions so the recipient will know how to use your gift. Lots of beautiful blank and decorative self-adhesive labels are available to accent your jars and decorate recipe cards. A laminating machine makes it easy to create practical, durable recipe cards - just print out the recipe on the computer or hand letter, laminate, punch a hole in the corner, and hang on the jar with gold elastic cord.

If you're making lots of jars for gifts, gang up recipe instructions on one sheet for cost-saving reproduction at the copy shop.

## Storing Culinary Mixes

Cool, dry storage is best. **Never** store finished jars near a heat source, hot pipes, stove, or furnace or in direct sunlight. If you cannot guarantee cool and dry storage, it's better to store your mixes in the refrigerator.

One excellent quality of your homemade mixes is that they are preservative-free. For maximum freshness, label them with a "best before" date.

### GENERAL TIPS FOR PACKAGING HOMEMADE MIXES

- Layer ingredients in the jar in the order given in the recipe.

- Wipe down the sides of the jar with a clean paper towel after adding powdery ingredients, such as powdered (icing) sugar, cocoa, or flour before adding the next ingredient for a better appearance.

- Pack down all ingredients firmly. If you don't, you won't have enough space to fit in all the ingredients. (You will be surprised at how flour packs down!) Generally, a quart jar holds 6 cups of packed down ingredients; a pint jar holds 3 cups of packed down ingredients. This is, however, a very general observation, as each recipe is made up of different ingredients that all pack down differently.

- If your ingredients do not come to the top of the jar, fill with crumpled plastic wrap or wax paper to prevent the ingredients from shifting and mixing.

Many factors determine the "best before" date, such as the type of flour (all-purpose flour has a longer shelf life than whole-wheat flour), preserving method (freshly dried herbs from your garden verses dried herbs bought from the market), and

This jar is filled with Caramel Corn made from the recipe in this section.

This is a great idea to send as a "care" package to a college student.

For instructions to decorate jar, see page 21.

the general quality and freshness of the ingredients you use. These factors have been taken in account when suggesting these recommended best-before dates:

- Dressing, dip, and seasoning blends - 6 months
- Beans, dried vegetable soup blends - 3 months
- Bread, muffin, and scone mixes - 2 weeks in the refrigerator
- Cookie and cake mixes - 2 months; with nuts - 1 month
- Coffee and tea mixes - 3 months

Even though many mixes would last much longer than the suggested times, the strength of the colors and flavors will fade. The goal is to provide foods that are both safe and of high quality. Remember *quality* is not the same as *safety*. A poor-quality food (such as stale cereal) may be safe to eat; an unsafe food may look and taste good but contain harmful bacteria.

## Substitutions

- Low-fat mayonnaise can be substituted for regular mayonnaise.
- Yogurt can be substituted for sour cream.
- Decaffeinated instant coffee can be substituted for regular instant coffee.

Mix Recipe

# Hot Cocoa Mix

*Makes 5-1/2 cups of mix.*

**Ingredients**
3 cups powdered milk
One 5-oz. pkg. non-instant chocolate pudding mix
1/2 cup powdered non-dairy creamer
1/4 cup unsweetened cocoa powder
1/4 cup powdered sugar

**Mix Instructions**
Layer all ingredients, in the order listed, in a quart-size canning jar.

Recipe Instructions

# Cup of Cocoa

Stir contents of jar before measuring. Add 1 heaping tablespoon Hot Cocoa Mix to 1 cup boiling water.

Recipe Instructions

# Cup of Spiced Tea

Stir contents of jar before measuring. Place 2 teaspoons of mix in a mug. Add 3/4 cup boiling water.

Mix Recipe

# Spiced Tea Mix

*Makes 1-1/2 cups of mix.*

**Ingredients**
1/2 cup powdered lemonade mix (unsweetened)
1/2 cup sugar
1/2 cup instant tea granules (unsweetened)
1/2 teaspoon cinnamon

**Instructions**
Layer all ingredients, in order listed, in a pint-size canning jar.

Warm a friend's heart with a gift of this charming snowflake jar
filled with hot cocoa mix. For instructions to decorate
Sparkly Snowflake Jar, see page 90.

111

Mix Recipe

# Cranberry Chocolate Cookie Mix

*Makes 4 cups of mix*

**Ingredients**
1-1/2 cups flour
1/2 teaspoon baking soda
1/2 teaspoon salt
1/2 cup rolled oats (not instant)
1/3 cup brown sugar, packed
1/3 cup sugar
1/2 cup dried cranberries
1/2 cup chocolate morsels
1/2 cup pecans

**Instructions**
Layer all ingredients, in order listed, in a quart-size canning jar. ❏

Recipe Instructions

# Cranberry Chocolate Cookies

*Makes 3 dozen cookies*

**Ingredients**
1 jar Cranberry Chocolate Cookie Mix
3/4 cup butter
1 large egg
2 teaspoons vanilla

**Instructions**
1. Preheat oven to 350 degrees F.
2. Cream butter, egg, and vanilla in a medium bowl until fluffy.
3. Add contents one jar of Cranberry Chocolate Cookie Mix. Mix well.
4. Drop by heaping tablespoons on greased cookie sheets. Bake for 15 minutes. ❏

The jar on the right contains the makings for Cranberry Chocolate Cookies.

For instructions to decorate Lacy Lids Jars, see page 16.

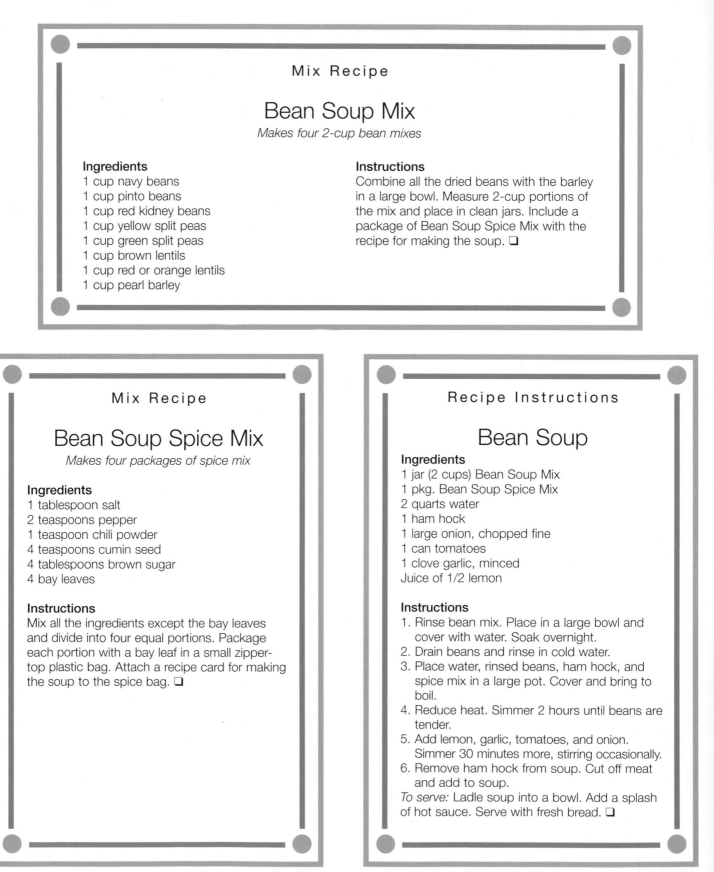

## Mix Recipe

# Bean Soup Mix

*Makes four 2-cup bean mixes*

**Ingredients**
1 cup navy beans
1 cup pinto beans
1 cup red kidney beans
1 cup yellow split peas
1 cup green split peas
1 cup brown lentils
1 cup red or orange lentils
1 cup pearl barley

**Instructions**
Combine all the dried beans with the barley in a large bowl. Measure 2-cup portions of the mix and place in clean jars. Include a package of Bean Soup Spice Mix with the recipe for making the soup. ❑

## Mix Recipe

# Bean Soup Spice Mix

*Makes four packages of spice mix*

**Ingredients**
1 tablespoon salt
2 teaspoons pepper
1 teaspoon chili powder
4 teaspoons cumin seed
4 tablespoons brown sugar
4 bay leaves

**Instructions**
Mix all the ingredients except the bay leaves and divide into four equal portions. Package each portion with a bay leaf in a small zipper-top plastic bag. Attach a recipe card for making the soup to the spice bag. ❑

## Recipe Instructions

# Bean Soup

**Ingredients**
1 jar (2 cups) Bean Soup Mix
1 pkg. Bean Soup Spice Mix
2 quarts water
1 ham hock
1 large onion, chopped fine
1 can tomatoes
1 clove garlic, minced
Juice of 1/2 lemon

**Instructions**
1. Rinse bean mix. Place in a large bowl and cover with water. Soak overnight.
2. Drain beans and rinse in cold water.
3. Place water, rinsed beans, ham hock, and spice mix in a large pot. Cover and bring to boil.
4. Reduce heat. Simmer 2 hours until beans are tender.
5. Add lemon, garlic, tomatoes, and onion. Simmer 30 minutes more, stirring occasionally.
6. Remove ham hock from soup. Cut off meat and add to soup.
*To serve:* Ladle soup into a bowl. Add a splash of hot sauce. Serve with fresh bread. ❑

*See page 96 for instructions to make the Bean Soup Jar.*

Mix Recipe

# Chicken Noodle Soup Mix

**Ingredients**
1 cup uncooked fine egg noodles
2 Tablespoons chicken bouillon
1/2 teaspoon pepper
1/4 teaspoon thyme
1/8 teaspoon celery seeds
1/8 teaspoon garlic powder
1 bay leaf

**Instructions**
Combine all ingredients and place in
a jar. ❑

Recipe Instructions

# Chicken Noodle Soup

**Ingredients**
1 jar Chicken Noodle Soup Mix
8 cups water
2 carrots, diced
2 stalks celery, diced
1/4 cup minced onion
3 cups cooked chicken meat

**Instructions**
1. Place all the ingredients except
   the chicken meat in a pot. Simmer
   for about 15 minutes.
2. Add the chicken meat and cook
   for 5 minutes. ❑

This beautiful lacy jar on the left is filled with the makings for Chicken Soup (see recipe in this section). This would be a lovely gift for a sick friend. The jar on the right is filled with Spiced Tea Mix. For instructions to create Lacy Lids Jars, see pages 16 and 17.

### Recipe

# Homemade Granola
*Makes 5 cups - 10 half-cup servings*

**Ingredients**
2 cups rolled oats (not instant)
1 cup shredded coconut
1/2 cup *each* chopped almonds,
chopped hazelnuts
1/2 cup wheat germ
2 tablespoons brown sugar
1/2 teaspoon cinnamon
1/2 cup honey
1/4 cup oil
1 cup dried fruit (cranberries, chopped
apricots, chopped apples, chopped
dates)

**Instructions**
1. Combine oats, coconut, nuts, wheat germ, brown sugar, and cinnamon.
2. Combine honey and oil. Stir into mixture.
3. Spread in a 9" x 13" baking pan.
4. Place in oven set to 300 degrees F. Bake until light golden brown, 40 to 50 minutes, stirring every 15 minutes.
5. Remove from oven. Stir in dried fruit. Place on another pan to cool.
6. Pack in jars. ❑

### Recipe

# Chocolate Candy

**Ingredients**
4 ounces unsweetened chocolate
1/2 cup corn syrup
1/3 cup raisins
1/2 cup hazelnuts or almonds, finely
chopped
1 teaspoon rum flavoring

**Instructions**
1. In a microwave oven or double boiler, melt chocolate.
2. Add corn syrup, raisins, rum flavoring, and nuts. Combine well.
3. Use two spoons to drop rounded spoonfuls on wax paper.
4. Refrigerate 30 minutes. Store in a glass jar. ❑

The Butterfly Jar on the left is filled with nutritious homemade granola. Pair it with the
Honey Bee Jar filled with honey and you have a great breakfast treat for a friend.
See page 27 for instructions on decorating jars.

Recipe

# Caramel Nut Popcorn
*Makes 6 cups*

## Ingredients
2 cups sugar
2 cups light brown sugar, firmly packed
2 cups light cream
1 teaspoon soft butter
3/4 teaspoon vanilla
1/4 cup *each* whole almonds and pecans
6 cups popped popcorn, all unpopped kernels removed

## Instructions
1. Combine sugars and cream in a saucepan. Stir until sugar is dissolved. Boil, uncovered, without stirring until syrup reaches softball stage (235-240 degrees F.)
2. Let cool 10 minutes, then beat with a wooden spoon until thickened.
3. Add vanilla and nuts and popcorn. Mix well.
4. Pour on sheets of parchment paper to cool. Break apart larger pieces before packaging in jars. ❑

Recipe

# Sugar & Spice Nuts
*Makes 4 cups*

## Ingredients
1/2 cup brown sugar
1/2 cup sugar
1 teaspoon cinnamon
1/2 teaspoon ginger
1/2 teaspoon nutmeg
1 egg white
1 tablespoon water
1 teaspoon vanilla
4 cups pecans

## Instructions
1. Preheat oven to 325 degrees F.
2. Combine sugars and spices.
3. Beat egg white with water until frothy. Combine with sugar and spice mixture. Add nuts. Stir.
4. Spread on a greased baking sheet. Bake 20 minutes, stirring occasionally, until dry looking and slightly browned. Let cool before packaging in jars. ❑

Fill Cork Tassel Jar or the Classic Jar with Sugar & Spice nuts for a much appreciated hostess gift. For jar decorating instructions, see page 26.

# Making Layered Culinary Mixes with Your Favorite Recipes

Consider developing your own layered mixes from your favorite recipes!
Here are some considerations:

• Will the ingredients look attractive in a jar?

• Can all the dry ingredients be mixed together or do you need to do a flavoring package (a separate packet of spices or dried herbs)?

• Will it fit into a quart jar? Pint jar?

• What else might be added to the recipe to make the mix more interesting or better looking? (E.g., colorful candy-coated chocolate candies instead of chocolate morsels)

• What could you use for the recipe that would also be a fun accent for the jar? (E.g., mini bottle of hot sauce, mixing spoon, wooden scoop)

• Always test your mixes before making them as gifts. Write the instructions for making your mix and attach it to the jar for easy reference.

## BEST TYPES OF RECIPES FOR GIFT MIXES

**Quick breads**
(muffins, pancakes, or scones)

**Cookies**

**Soups**

**Drink mixes**
(hot chocolate, tea blends, or instant tea)

*Pictured right:*
Natural Storage
Canisters, page 52.

Fragrance Recipe

# Baby Yourself Bath Salts

*This recipe makes 2 jars of salts but could easily be doubled or tripled. Candy sprinkles add fun and color to the salts and dissolve quickly in the bath.*

**Ingredients**
2 cups Epsom salts
Yellow and green soap colorants
10 drops lemon fragrance oil
10 drops peppermint fragrance oil
1 tablespoon candy sprinkles

**Instructions**
1. Place 1 cup salt in each of two glass jars. To one jar, add 4 drops yellow colorant, lemon fragrance oil, and candy sprinkles. To jar two, add 3 drops green colorant and 5 drops peppermint fragrance oil.
2. Place the lids on the jars. Shake well to distribute the color and fragrance. Leave in the jars for 24 hours.
3. Package the salts in pint jars, alternating a layers from jar one and jar two.

*To use:*
Draw a warm bath and add the fragrant salts to the running water. Hop in and relax, inhaling deeply to experience the refreshing and soothing aroma. ❑

Bath Time Jar, see page 22 for decorating instructions.

# Metric Conversion Chart

## Inches to Millimeters and Centimeters

| Inches | MM | CM |
|--------|-----|------|
| 1/8 | 3 | .3 |
| 1/4 | 6 | .6 |
| 3/8 | 10 | 1.0 |
| 1/2 | 13 | 1.3 |
| 5/8 | 16 | 1.6 |
| 3/4 | 19 | 1.9 |
| 7/8 | 22 | 2.2 |
| 1 | 25 | 2.5 |
| 1-1/4 | 32 | 3.2 |
| 1-1/2 | 38 | 3.8 |
| 1-3/4 | 44 | 4.4 |
| 2 | 51 | 5.1 |
| 3 | 76 | 7.6 |
| 4 | 102 | 10.2 |
| 5 | 127 | 12.7 |
| 6 | 152 | 15.2 |
| 7 | 178 | 17.8 |
| 8 | 203 | 20.3 |
| 9 | 229 | 22.9 |
| 10 | 254 | 25.4 |
| 11 | 279 | 27.9 |
| 12 | 305 | 30.5 |

## Yards to Meters

| Yards | Meters |
|-------|--------|
| 1/8 | .11 |
| 1/4 | .23 |
| 3/8 | .34 |
| 1/2 | .46 |
| 5/8 | .57 |
| 3/4 | .69 |
| 7/8 | .80 |
| 1 | .91 |
| 2 | 1.83 |
| 3 | 2.74 |
| 4 | 3.66 |
| 5 | 4.57 |
| 6 | 5.49 |
| 7 | 6.40 |
| 8 | 7.32 |
| 9 | 8.23 |
| 10 | 9.14 |

# Index

*Continued on next page*

# Index